The Island of Memes:
Haiti's Unfinished Revolution

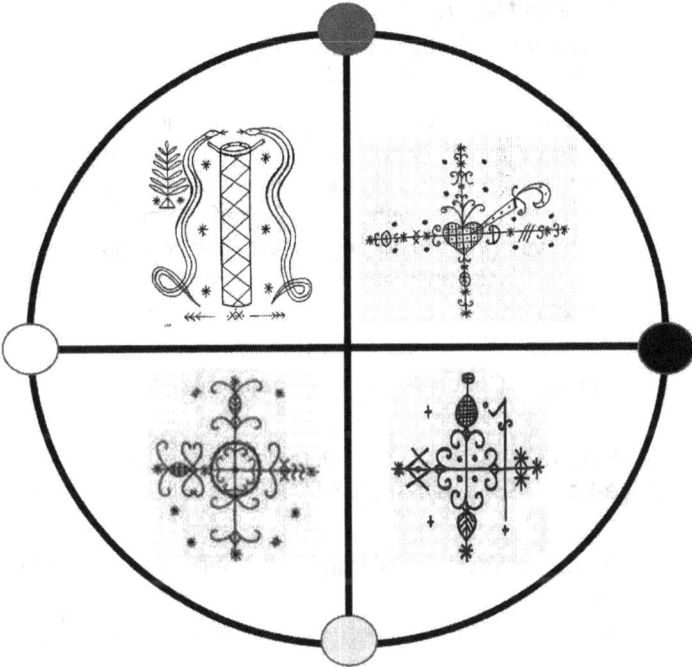

Wade W. Nobles
Ifagbemi Sangodare Nana Kwaku Berko I Bejana Onebunne

Dedicated to

Syed Khatib
Kimbwandende Kia Bunseki Fu-Kiau

and

Francois Mackandal
Dutty Boukman
Cecile Fatima
Toussaint L'Ouverture
Jean Jacque Dessalines

Explanation of the cover design:

Designed by the author, the cover represents the combining of the Dikenga dia Kongo (BaNtu-Kongo cosmogram) with the four Vodou vévés. Dikenga dia Kongo symbolizes the four moments of the sun (four phases of life's passage) and the Kongo emblem of spiritual continuity and renaissance. The four Vodou vévés, believed to be significant in sparking the Haitian revolution, at the Bos Caimen ceremony were the Lwa's of Legba, Damballa, Simbi and Erzulie Dante. Vévés represent astral forces or energy. During the course of spiritual ceremonies, the reproduction/representation of astral forces/energy as a Vévé calls or obliges particular spirits (Lwa) to come from the invisible realm to the visible realm.

Table of Contents

Foreword

Dr. Wade Nobles has made a fundamental and critically needed contribution to the new intellectual discourse that is necessary to understand the past, dissect the present, and project a meaningful future. *The Island of Memes: Haiti's Unfinished Revolution* is in the best tradition of African scholarship and scientific research, which describes, analyzes, and then prescribes a way forward, a plan of action and a cure. African-centered scholars in this tradition include Chancellor Williams, who published the outstanding masterpiece *The Destruction of Black Civilization* and later *The Rebirth of African Civilization*; John Henrik Clarke contributed a classic work entitled *Notes for an African World Revolution: Africans at the Crossroads*; Asa Hilliard contributed *The Maroon Within Us: Selected Essays on African American Community Socialization*; Jacob Carruthers added his powerful *Intellectual Warfare.*

"Pan-Africanism or perish" was the formidable statement about Africa's destiny often stated by Master-Teacher Dr. John Henrik Clarke, who was a pioneer scholar in establishing Africana Studies; organizing associations of scholars, teachers, and researchers; and creating think-tanks and research institutes. He was the foremost inspiration for linking the African Diaspora and the continent of Africa. His greatest work was entitled *Notes for an African World Revolution: Africans at the Crossroads* in which he analyzed the incomplete revolutions of Marcus Garvey, Patrice Lumumba, Kwame Nkrumah, Malcolm X, and Tom Mboya. He called upon Africans to complete the work started by these visionaries.

Dr. Clarke inspired many of us to contribute to the Great Awakening of African Peoples after World War II and join in the Pan-African crusade. Among those so inspired were Dr. Jacob Carruthers, Dr. Asa Hilliard, and the author, Dr. Wade Nobles, who accepted the mantle of leadership in Africana Studies and proceeded to establish a monumental model of "illuminating" African greatness in spite of the "shattered consciousness and fractured identity." This extraordinary work represents an historic formulation for past, current, and future studies of our nation-building and community development.

9

This historic and timely interplay of mutual stimulation between the African Diasporan family and Continental Africans must be encouraged and institutionalized and certainly systematized. The results of this interplay have been monumental and extraordinarily productive. No better example of the mutual stimuli and interplay can be found than the relationship of love and respect and mutual admiration and inspiration that became a reality between Dr. Cheikh Anta Diop and the Diasporans. From his great work entitled *Black Africa: The Economic and Cultural Basis for a Federated State* to his classic publication *The Cultural Unity of Africa* to his magnum opus *Civilization or Barbarism*, the mutual stimuli has unleashed a flow of knowledge and creative genius that has provided the African Global Family with the basis for victory in the cultural, intellectual, and spiritual wars for control of the African mind/mine.

The relationship has been replicated by Dr. Diop's comrade-in-arms and colleague in the great war for the mind of Africans, Dr. Theophile Obenga, who has shared his expertise and vision with the Congo-Brazza School of African Knowledge, The Paris School, the Temple University Philadelphia School, and the Bay Area School. He is currently helping to build a Pan-African University in Brazzaville, Republic of the Congo. His definitive works include *African Philosophy: The Pharaonic Period 2700-300 BC* and a key role as part of the UNESCO team that produced the ground-breaking eight-volume *General History of Africa*. Another example of the interplay and mutual stimulation in this Pan-African whirlwind is a scholar-professor-traditional Chief of Ghana, West Africa, Nana Kobina Nketsia V, who has recently published a remarkable and surely needed masterpiece, entitled *African Culture in Governance and Development: The Ghana Paradigm*. This work is an extraordinary example of the power of the intellectual, cultural, and spiritual interplay between the African Diasporans and the Continentals.

The BaNtu-Kongo area of Central Africa has also produced an outstanding and unique scholar-warrior-elder Dr. Kia Bunseki Fu-Kiau whose wisdom and knowledge of KiKongo deep thought has informed and stimulated Diasporan scholars for decades, notably Dr. Asa Hilliard and the author, Dr. Wade Nobles. Among his many

works is his masterpiece *African Cosmology of the BaNtu-Kongo*.
Dr. Nobles synthesizes the indigenous knowledge of Dr. Fu-Kiau
and further explores his concept of "Tornadoes of the Mind."

It is truly a question of Pan-Africanism and the African Renaissance, the prophetic theme chosen by African leaders in the African
Union to represent this decisive moment in our history. Upon this African foundation, we are called by the Divine Order, the ancestors,
and the creators of our Deep Thought to build the African future.
This brilliant achievement by Diasporan Africans is a necessary and
critical stimulant to the work that must be accomplished by our best
minds. It is clear, however, that the heavy lifting must be done by
Continental Africans who are immersed in the Mother culture. And
no matter how much it has been dislocated, devastated and destroyed, it is the definitive foundation upon which we must build.

The explosion of African nations joining the global community
has been one of the most astonishing events of the twentieth century and represents a turning point in world history. The period from
1945 to 1995 has been unmatched in terms of change, transformation, rebirth, and regeneration. From the 5th Pan-African Conference in Manchester, England, in the Fall of 1945 after World War II
through the liberation struggles up to the election of Nelson Mandela in 1994, there has been an unprecedented economic, political,
and cultural African Global Revolution that has produced more than
fifty new nations, which are independent states, organized initially in
1963 into the Organization of African Unity and later into the African
Union.

The roots of this explosion, however, are found in the extraordinary earth shattering events two hundred years ago on the island
of Hispaniola, later called Haiti. The African Revolution in Haiti
exploded on the world scene in the same historical period as the
American and French Revolutions and unleashed a whirlwind of
economic, political, and cultural power whose ramifications are still
being felt worldwide. This unique role of the Haitian Revolution must
be seriously studied as a model of what victories can happen when
Africans organize around African Spirituality and what devastation
can result from the reactions of the systems of white supremacy.

Dr. Wade Nobles and his colleagues have provided the African world with a template that can be utilized to heal the shattered consciousness and fractured identity of the Global African Family.

Professor Nobles has brilliantly revisited the history involving Africans in Haiti and their relationship to Europe and America. He has applied his knowledge of African psychology to the unfolding drama of the human family and provided the world with a template by which one can better understand the broader human manifestations. History is not just an episode; it is the unfolding of the human family on planet earth and in the cosmos. The role of Africa, Africans, and Africaness in this cosmic drama is often not understood or appreciated and is too often purposefully distorted, dismissed, denigrated, and manipulated as part of the systems of de-Africanization and de-humanization of African peoples. This is a critical juncture in African History, and every thought and action has the potential for becoming liberating or incarcerating. There is great need for understanding the task of understanding, being, becoming, and belonging. We must create the context of our own growth and development. We need deep, profound and penetrating search, study, understanding, and mastery of the illumination of the African spirit in our time and place. We must become "Sakhu Djaerist."

This exceptional study by Wade Nobles is the result of decades of research and praxis around the African World in an attempt to apply the knowledge and understanding of African-centered psychology. He believes there is a need to transform psychology, particularly, African psychology whose role is the mental liberation of African people. For this great scholar, culture is the key factor. He firmly states that "it is in the reclamation of our culture and ancient African thought, and in the creative reconstruction of them as African psychology, that Black people can regain control over the interpretation of our reality and the process of our human development." His experiences in Haiti after the devastating earthquake on January 12, 2010, as part of the Association of Black Psychologists Disaster Relief Task Force, prepared him and other associates and colleagues to rethink their approaches to assisting the Haitian people. Dr. Wade Nobles has stated prophetically, "The deep thinkers of the African world are on the brink of reclaiming a system of thinking and doing that cannot fall victim to non-African cultural hegemony and intellectual domination." The genius of Wade Nobles' monumental work is that it illuminates the African culture and spirit while it dissects the deep psychological dimensions of the struggle and exposes the contradictions of the Euro-Asian- Arab systems of development that contribute to the devastation and genocide of African peoples.

In this work Dr. Nobles has provided the African world with a new direction. It is both insightful and radical, insightful because it takes the reader to a new and unique way of understanding the agents and agency that determine our contemporary lives. It is radical in that it goes deep into the root form of African consciousness that shapes our being and becoming. This is a bold and ambitious contribution to the African offensive in the current "Cultural Wars" that are at the center of the struggle for the African mind/mine. It provides the necessary new intellectual discourse in the understanding of human psychology, cultural studies, traditional African spirituality, political science, and race relations. Furthermore, this work allows those responsible for the development of indigenous peoples to access a deeper African consciousness in order to produce processes that will result in economic, political, and cultural systems that are truly designed to serve African peoples. *The Island of Memes: Haiti's Unfinished Revolution* includes a prescription and cure and explains the need for a restoration project not just for the unfinished Revolution in the Republic of Haiti, but the unfinished revolutions throughout the African world.

—Dr. Leonard Jeffries (Dr. J.)
President,
World African Diaspora Union (WADU)

Acknowledgements

As acknowledgement, I must first and foremost recognize Syed Khatib and Kimbwandende Kia Bunseki Fu-Kiau. Syed Khatib transitioned into the abode of the ancestors during the completion of this manuscript. Professor Khatib was my teacher, and like Asa Hilliard and Jake Carruthers, he dwelled, while alive, in the area of my closest and best friendships. Syed ignited in me and Phil (McGee) and Na'im (Akbar) an undying thirst for finding critical scholarship and uncompromising excellence in the ideas, beliefs, and thinking of Africa. Syed read the first rough draft of this manuscript, and as with our earlier collaborations through the Society of African Sciences (SAAS), he provided inspiration along with a clear and strong critique of the necessary coherence needed in thought and comprehension for this narrative.

Preceding Syed in joining Jake and Asa amongst the dwellers of heaven, Dr. Bunseki Fu-Kiau stoked and further fueled that very same fire of African grounded scholarship and excellence. Ya Fu-kiau guided and cautioned me to go slowly and to be deliberate in the reclamation of African ideas and the restoration of the African mind. Particularly for this manuscript, he tutored me in the concepts and thoughts most relevant to questions of consciousness and the fracturing of the African mind. Through our talks, he allowed me to see a living example of what it means to be a scholar-healer. Just being in his presence and absorbing his calm teachings elevated me and my sense of the possible. He honored me as *"Ganga Nganga"* and taught us all *"Simba Simbi."* I am and will be forever shaped by our conversations and collaboration. Next, I wish to thank my editors, Ms. Apryl Motley and Ms. Marcia Cross-Briscoe, without whose technical skills this book would have not found itself completed and deserving of print.

The birth of this book, in actuality, would have not happened if Dr. Gislene Mariette and Dr. Mary Elizabeth Hargrow had not agreed to co-chair, with me, the Association of Black Psychologists' Disaster Relief Task Force. They, like me, were deployed to Haiti shortly after the earthquake to make a first-hand assessment of the mental health recovery efforts needed. Part of our

17

charge was also to author The ABPsi Disaster Restoration Series: Culturally Congruent (African Centered) Mental Health Services and Programming for African Ancestry Victims of Natural and/or Man-made Disasters Manual. As an ongoing collaborative process to complete the manual, I benefited from engagement with both Gislene and Mary Elizabeth's thoughts and ideas. It was the experience of being in Haiti and this dialog that served as immediate inspiration for the idea of this book. I am thankful to both Gislene and Mary Elizabeth. I also must acknowledge the many people in Haiti who informed my insights. While visiting the AZN camp, a young 16 year-old girl, Norvely Antoine, who was serving as the camp secretary, calmly and efficiently told us that there were 6074 people there, including 1584 families and 1069 children between the ages of 0-18 and that she was part of a group of young Black Haitians who were managing this particular camp.

In walking amongst the disaster, I remember watching a little Haitian boy, who was playing with a broken toy trumpet and imagining the sound of music. While his home had been destroyed and his parents most likely killed, his spirit of creativity was not destroyed by the earthquake. I am thankful to Norvely, her compatriots, and the many unnamed Haitian children for showing me a living example of the Haitian revolutionary consciousness. During this visit, I also benefited from sitting and dialoging with two extraordinary Haitian psychologists, Marjory Clermont Mathieu and Ronald Jean Jacques. Without their initial seeding, there would have been no fruit to bear, and I am thankful.

From the time I returned from Haiti to the submission of this manuscript, the continuous dialogs and briefing held with The Institute for the Advanced Study of Black Family Life and Culture, Inc.'s staff, scholars-in-residence, and employees helped me in immeasurable ways to shape the thinking found in this text. I am thankful without limit to Dr. Lawford L. Goddard, Dr. Rachel Bernard Cooks, Amara Benjamin-Bullock, Sureshi Jayawardene, Clarence George III, Dr. Serie McDougal, Monika Scott-Davis, Alexandra Munson, Takiya Smith, Dawn Edwards, and Michael Nobles. I also want to acknowledge Dr. Leonard Jeffries, Professor James Smalls, and Bayyinah Bello. They helped me, without even knowing it, to comprehend the idea of a complex cache of consciousness and the simultaneous need for clarity. Without their insights, comments, and intellectual offerings, there would be no book. Thank you all so very much.

I also would like to give particular thanks and acknowledgement to a special group of men and women whom I respectfully refer to as practitioners of "spirit science" or "Spirit Talkers." They, in their generosity, helped me to reflect deeply on the African way of being. These Spirit Beings in the form (bodies) of the Araba of Osogbo, Nigeria, Baba Ifayemi Elebuibon; the traditional priest, Nana Kwabena Abebresse Abass (Nana Alhaji Abass) of Ghana; the Ndepp of Senegal, Oulimata Diop; the High Sanusi of South Africa, Baba Credo Mutwa; the Sangoma Mama Virginia; and the Nganga of the Congo, Kimwandende Kia Bunseki Fu-kiau, helped me to peek into the deep well of African traditional epistemology. Guided by ongoing direct conversations and study with these practitioners of African spirit science (religion), I am becoming a better "Sakhu Djaerist." I am eternally indebted to them.

Finally, I wish to unashamedly give the greatest thanks to my wife, Dr. Vera L. Nobles. Neither *The Island of Memes* nor any other work I have ever written would have been presented to the public without Vera's keen critique, thoughtful intellectual sensibilities, and invaluable cultural and spiritual guidance. Her support has given me the ability to go beyond my own self-imposed intellectual limitations. She, more than anyone else, knows the depth of my gratitude. To Vera Lynn Winmilawe Nokwanda, forever and a day after eternity, I will be thankful for your gifts.

The usefulness and value of this book belong to all those abovementioned as well as to the ancestral spirits that have chosen to speak through me. Whatever limitations or faults found in and on these pages, I am solely responsible.

Introduction

..... National liberation struggle is a revolution that is not over at the moment when the flag is hoisted and the national anthem is played.
—Amilcar Cabral, Unity and Struggle[1] (1979)

The forms and functions of psychological operations are considered universal and thus can be found in all cultures and societies. However, aspects of mental processes associated with the human mind should be thought of as distinct and particular to the various cultural communities found in human society. Accordingly, the power and functioning of the mind and psyche can be viewed as cultural formations and expressions peculiar to particular peoples. The psychological understandings, theoretical applications, and therapeutic interventions must all be consistent with the cultural meaning of the people being examined. Every aspect of the human experience—from habilitate to rehabilitate—must be culturally congruent if an accurate psychological understanding is to be achieved.

Consequently, this work is guided by the additional belief that a critical task and challenge of the African-centered scholar/intellectual is to identify and promote the interests and image of Africa and Africa's children by understanding the past, present, and future of our human story through the Africanization of the epistemological, terminological, aesthetic, and hermeneutical groundings of the scientific, artistic and investigative discourse. Likewise, the African-centered psychologist must simultaneously understand the past, present, and future of Africa and Africa's children and center the analytical, therapeutic process, and rehabilitative discourse in an African episteme and praxis.

Using the Haitian Revolution as a case study exemplar, this manuscript examines Haiti at a critical period in time to discuss the role consciousness and identity played in its liberation struggle and the formation of nationhood. In asserting itself as an independent and authentic scientific discipline, Black psychology is utilized, herein, to understand not only the Haitian mind in conflict but the African mind struggling for liberation worldwide.

Having the distinction of being the first independent nation in Latin America and the first Black-led republic in the world, today Haiti is considered the poorest country in the Americas as per the Human Development Index.[2] Maligned by the misunderstanding and fear of its African spiritual beliefs and the adoption of forced religious and economic impositions, Haiti has experienced foreign interference and political violence from its very inception and throughout its history.

On January 12, 2010, Haiti experienced a 7.0 magnitude earthquake that devastated Port-au-Prince with immeasurable destruction and resulted in an immediate death count estimated to be greater than 220,000 men, women, and children. Shortly after the earthquake, I was deployed to Haiti as part of the Association of Black Psychologists Disaster Relief Task Force. Our specific charge was to determine how the ABPsi could assist in identifying Black psychology principles, best practices, and strategies, which would allow for the illumination and liberation of the Haitian spirit and assist Haitian people in addressing the psychological trauma and mental stress associated with this tragedy, past traumas, and the rebirthing of the Haitian family, nation, and psyche. It was during this visit that I became acutely aware of the complexity of class, gender, and skin color privilege that was, in my opinion, the unspoken impediment to Haiti's recovery and post-earthquake development.

This text grew out of my desire to understand the historical source and current consequence of Haiti's special history and mentality. It is written to underscore the Haitian historical—and more importantly, psychological—quest for liberty that as an experiential cauldron seeded and shaped the power and function of the contemporary Haitian mind. The formation of Haiti's complex consciousness and identity can serve as a case study and an explanatory template for African people throughout the African world, both continental and Diasporan. Consequently, in the analysis of Haitian reality, the application of Black psychology is essential to our understanding of the complexities and contradictions experienced as Haitian consciousness.

The Island of Memes: Haiti's Unfinished Revolution is more than the traditional psychohistory or historical narrative. This book is a radical blending of the historical birth of the first independent Black nation with innovative analyses of the roles of consciousness formation and fragmentation seen through the lens of Black psychology.

The concept of *Sakhu Sheti/Djaer*, as a further refinement and deeper extension of Black psychology's African essence, is discussed extensively in the book.[3] It was introduced in my work in 1986.[4] *Sakhu Djaer/Sheti* is the process of understanding, examining, and explicating the meaning, nature, and functioning of being human for African people by conducting a deep, profound, and penetrating search, study, and mastery of the process of illuminating the human spirit or essence and experience. *Sakhu Sheti* represents an investigative approach that requires a penetrating search, study, and understanding of phenomena that seeks the deeper meaning of phenomena and explores every (including the unseen) aspect of reality. The task of illuminating African consciousness is complex. *Sakhu Djaer/Sheti* is presented as a key intellectual charge for this discourse.

This work is part of a continuous effort to provide a new intellectual discourse in the understanding of human psychology, cultural studies, traditional African spirituality, political science, and race relations. It is a specific attempt to illuminate the shaping of consciousness in the cauldron of political turmoil and social formation as psycho-cultural and geopolitical legacy in current human relations and contemporary world affairs. The timeliness of this discussion is embedded in both the worldwide response to the human tragedy associated with the earthquake in Haiti and the ever-evolving worldwide economic crises that are shaping a new world ordering. The aftermath of Haiti's earthquake brought the human family from around the world together to help a country shattered by repeated man-made disasters only to be further torn asunder by a natural disaster. Haiti's African consciousness as understood through an African episteme directs this discourse. The clash of humanity in Haiti serves as an important opportunity for all of us to attempt to fathom how privilege, class, gender, culture, race, religion, and caste must be fully understood as questions of consciousness and humanity.

In the brief opening chapter, the concept of Sakhu/Djaer as a further refinement of Black psychology's African essence and the role of the Black psychologist as a Sakhu practitioner is discussed. A Sakhu/Djaer methodology is offered as an innovative praxis for reviewing the psychology of dehumanization and the investigatory method for revisiting the question of Haiti's unfinished revolution as a complex cache of conflicting consciousness.

Chapter II illustrates through Black psychology the damaging impact of colonialism and chattel slavery on the minds and consciousness of African people victimized by these historical movements. In this chapter the concept of "meme," sensoria-information structure or contagious information patterns that replicate by symbiotically infecting human minds and altering behavior causing them to propagate the pattern, is introduced. The idea of "memetic infection" is also introduced. These sensoria-information structures can be in the form of symbols, images, feelings, words, ideas, customs, practices, or any knowable and perceptible item or substance. As sensorial information structures, memes are passed on from one generation to the next while preserving their core content or meaning and capacity to preserve the altered behavior. It is noted, in this chapter, that memetics would, in fact, suggest that the contagious information pattern that replicated itself in Haiti, via infecting the minds of the enslaved African, was an identifiable complex of ideas and experiences that supported the belief that the African was "chattel" and void of human value and worth, while an African memetic ideation offered a counter ideological position of "being" free and African.

Chapter III provides a further and first-time interpretation of the damaging impact of colonialism and chattel slavery on the minds and consciousness of African peoples. This chapter also discusses a clash of cultures and consciousness fueled by the ideology of white supremacy. The concept of "memes" as introduced is utilized as a theoretical template for understanding the derailment of African historical consciousness and identity. The experience of enslavement and Hispaniola's memetic infection are re-interrogated as psychological phenomena wherein the consciousness of Hispaniola (Haiti) is formed as a "memetic" confluence of European, African, and to a lesser extent, Arawak ideations and beliefs.

Chapter IV is the cornerstone chapter of this manuscript. It is dedicated to interrogating the enslavement experience and dynamics of bondage as a mental dialectic of consciousness between the master (European memetic ideations) and the enslaved (African memetic ideations). The essential role of African spirituality (i.e., BaNtu-Kongo) and the significance of the families of "nanchons" (nations), which were groupings of African spiritual forces, are re-analyzed as memetic ideations that fundamentally shaped the consciousness of the Haitian spirit. Each of the major Loa (transplanted African spirits), Boukman Dutty (master of the African spiritual force called Bo), and Cecile Fatiman (mother of the African spiritual force called Bo) are described, and their importance in the Bois Caimen ceremony is discussed. Particular attention is given to BaNtu-Kongo consciousness and meaning of being human and the enslaved African in Hispaniola being infected with European memes (ideations and beliefs). The question of liberty and freedom and the ensuing struggle are discussed in the context of a memetic legacy. The African struggle for liberation in Haiti is examined for the first time as a clash of psycho-cultural realities. The Vodu ceremony conducted at Bois Caimen (the Alligator Swamp) is analyzed in some detail to reveal both the African episteme and the spiritual system that activated the minds and behaviors of those African men and women whose will to be free led to the overthrow of the most powerful military force in the world.

Chapter V provides a discussion of consciousness grounded in African philosophy and worldview. This chapter further emphasizes the critical and essential role of African spiritual systems in the spark and success of the Haitian revolution. As a result, the Haitian revolution is re-examined as the cause and consequence of a cache of consciousness typified by and revealed in the lives and roles of the main architects (Toussaint, Dessalines, Christophe, and Petion) of the Haitian revolution.

In breaking away from the European notion of historiography, Chapter VI focuses on the role of key revolutionaries in the Haitian revolution (i.e., Toussaint L'Ouverture, Jean Jacque Dessalines, Henri Christophe, and Andre Sabes Petion) as their lives and contributions are examined as a cache of consciousness, which was shaped by the staunch reality of Haitian slavery while simultaneously shaping the reality and possibility of a liberated reality. In applying a Congo notion of "Tornados of the Mind," the lingering effects of colonialism and chattelization, which resulted in an invisible pervasive sense of human alienation and the distortion of African consciousness and identity, is discussed. The mental enslavement, shattered consciousness, and fractured identity, resulting from this historical memetic infection (in the form of class and caste), remain the driving force of modern Haitian society.

In the final chapter, the contemporary interplay of Haiti's shattered African consciousness and fractured Black identity as a structural barrier to the success of Haiti's enslaved Africans' desire to be fully free and African is also examined. The contemporary legacy of the conflicting consciousness is discussed in the aftermath of the destructive earthquake of 2010. In so doing, it is argued that Haiti's revolution remains unfinished. The ancient African concept of Serudja ta (restoration) is introduced as a template for the reciprocal re-birth (reparation) of the Haitian African character, psyche, and community.

---

[1]   As cited in Davidson, B. (1979). *Unity and Struggle: Speeches and Writings of Amilcar Cabral.*

[2]   See Haq, M. and Sen, A. (1990). *The Human Development Concept.*

[3] It should be noted that while I believe that the discipline of Black psychology will ultimately come to be referred to as "Sakhu Sheti," throughout this manuscript, Black psychology, African psychology, and African-centered psychology will be used interchangeably.

[4] See Nobles, W. (1986) "Ancient Egyptian Thought and the Development of African (Black) Psychology." In M. Karenga & J. H. Carruthers (Eds.), *Kemet and the African Worldview, Research, Rescue and Restoration* (pp. 100-118).

Chapter One

Sakhu Sheti, Black Psychology and the Psychology of Dehumanization

This discussion is rooted in the field of Black psychology.[1] As such, it is important at the outset to note that Black psychology is neither narrowly race-specific nor limited ethnically. Given this recognition, many Black psychologists have devoted their careers to developing Black psychological theory, therapy, and practice to address people of African ancestry's needs. Black psychology, as such, is grounded in the special, cultural, and philosophical fabric that defines the humanity of African people. The assumption is that people of African ancestry share certain orientations that are based on a common spiritual essence and similar cultural beliefs and practices as well as concrete historical experiences.

Black psychology, as it is being developed, is the self-conscious "centering" of psychological analyses and applications in African realities, cultures, and epistemologies. African-centered psychology, as a system of thought and action, examines the processes that allow for the illumination and liberation of the spirit. Relying on the principles of harmony within the universe as a natural order of existence, African-centered psychology recognizes that (1) spirit permeates everything; (2) everything in the universe is interconnected; (3) the collective is the most salient element of existence; and (4) communal self-knowledge is the key to mental health. African psychology is ultimately concerned with understanding the systems of meaning of being human, the features of human functioning, and the restoration of the normal/natural order of human development.

The psychological effect that the ideology of white supremacy and European imperialism, in the form of slavery and colonialism, has had on Africa and her people has never been fully addressed and understood. The development of the academic field of Black psychology has ushered in a new respect for the legitimacy of various ethnic conceptions of psychological functioning. In fact, Black psychology has forced the overall field of psychology to recognize that there is no universal psychiatric reality, and, in terms of psychological knowledge and practice, the only valid perspective is one that reflects the culture of the people served. No longer do functionalist paradigms, reflecting ideologies of western hegemonic healing methods and positivistic social science, stand as the universal model for all human communities. Simply put, there is no universal psychiatric reality.[2] Whether it is professional (modern) or folk (traditional), every aspect of psychological knowledge and practice is a reflection of the constructed world of a particular people.

Black Psychology, Dehumanization, and African Development

Black Psychology is intentionally formulated to be grounded in African philosophical thought and wisdom traditions. It is designed to be culturally congruent with the humanity of African people. Since a people's indigenous culture anchors them to reality, culture must be the starting point for all recovery, restoration, and understanding. It is believed that Black psychology is the critical discipline missing from the discourse on Africa's renaissance and development.

One constant imperative in Black psychology is the recognition of the damaging impact of colonialism and chattel enslavement on the African mind and consciousness. Recognition is coupled with a profound understanding that the meaning of being African, for both continental and diasporic Africans, is prescribed in the visible and invisible realms of reality. Yet our understanding of what it means to be African depends only on conceptions of material reality grounded in European thought. To be African is more than biology, sociology, or history. What makes us African is fundamentally spirit (ness) or essence (energy). It is an awareness of being spirit and that regardless of time and place, we are African.

Sakhu Djaer/Sheti

The early 70s saw the first introduction of African philosophy as the grounding for a new Black psychology.[3] During the next two decades, several Black psychologists[4] joined in the excavation of ancient African ideas as grounding for the re-emergence of a Black psychology. As part of this ongoing dialogue, in the late 90s, the concept of *Sakhu Sheti/Djaer* (Skh Sdi/Djr)[5], as a further refinement and deeper extension of Black psychology's African essence, was introduced.

Sakhu Djaer (Skh Djr) is the process of understanding, examining, and explicating the meaning, nature, and functioning of being human for African people. It is achieved by conducting a deep, profound, and penetrating search, thorough study, and mastery of the process of illuminating the human spirit or essence, as well as all human experience and phenomena. This process recognizes that a full understanding of reality acknowledges that spirit is the basis of all known and knowable phenomena and perceptions. The word Sdi means to save, to preserve, to recover, to rescue, to reserve, to dig, to remove, to pull, to recite, to keep safe, to break, to take away, to maintain, to exact, to collect, to hand over, to deliver, to levy, rob, and to steal. It has been suggested in this regard that the combining of Sku and Sdi, ergo, *"Skh Sdi,"* would reference the idea that human beings as spirit are led by Spirit, 'reads' spirit(s); seek help and protection from Spirit, and engage in the salvation and 'nurturing' (healing) of Spirit by performing the Sakhu as it should be done

In Black psychology, *Sakhu Sheti/Djaer*, as a penetrating search, study, and understanding, requires an investigative approach that always seeks the deeper meaning of phenomena and explores the invisible aspects of reality. As such, it requires a search for the deeper meaning of phenomena and explores every aspect of reality, including the unseen. Accordingly, psychological knowing and knowledge production must be guided by a different set of epistemological considerations. The notion of *Sakhu* informs both the episteme and the method. As episteme it gives recognition to the idea that (1) all phenomena of nature are symbolic writings, and hidden in the symbols are the forces and laws governing the material and spiritual aspects of the universe; (2) the symbol and symbolism should be understood as means for transmitting precise and exact rational and supra-rational knowledge linked to inner (intrinsic vision) reality, and (3) the material (visible) representation of the immaterial (invisible) qualities and functions of being are objectifications of things subjective in us and subliminal in nature.

The limitation that "thinking" alone has on simultaneously engaging the known (that which can be perceived), the unknown (that which cannot be perceived), and the beyond knowing (that which transcends thought) is addressed by *"Irt Skh"* (performing the illumination). As such the task of illuminating human reality is complex and requires the recognition and respect for the distinction between the realms of knowing and the levels of awareness (self-other perception and perception beyond the ordinary). The Sakhu investigatory method requires the illumination of the invisible in order to achieve "transformative-synchronistic-analogic" insight and modality. Hence, *"irt skh"* (performing the illumination) is to engage in a deep, profound, and penetrating search, study, understanding, and mastery of the process of illuminating the human spirit and reality by (1) clarifying our definition, meaning, and resolute position/purpose in the world, (2) analyzing and describing the concrete human conditions which affect and influence our collective human development and consciousness, and (3) prescribing and exciting solutions and actions, which will free African people from both material and spiritual degradation.

The paradigmatic praxis implied by *Sakhu* has real and important implications for the Black psychologist as a *"sakhu practitioner."* Specifically, the *"sakhu practitioner"* as researcher, teacher, theorist, therapist, or analyst, will be responsible for:

(1) Reflecting and protecting the human integrity of African people,

(2) Serving as a guide into and for the future growth and development of the humanity of African people,

(3) Drawing upon a source of energy and understanding that will ignite and enhance the spiritual, mental, and physical well-being of African people;

(4) Working to guarantee African liberation, intellectual enlightenment, and ongoing human development; and

(5) Becoming the stimulus for and evidence of the illumination of the African human spirit.

Slavery, Colonialism, and the Morphing of African Ideas and Being

While Haiti is being used as an exemplar case, the analyses of colonialism, slavery, and the morphing of African ideas and being throughout the Diaspora can be viewed through the prism or discipline of Black psychology and its further Africanization as Sakhu Djaer/Sheti. Throughout this text, *Sakhu Djaer/Sheti* will be presented as a key intellectual charge for this discourse on Haiti's unfinished revolution. Haiti, arguably, is the most African nation-state in the Western hemisphere, and its illumination (Skh Sdi) will provide greater insight and tools for excavating the content, contours, and context of African development worldwide.

Dating back to the earliest times, systems of human servitude, serfdom, slavery, and indentured labor were established. Slavery gained in economic importance after the 16th century with the European conquest of South and Central America. Slavery in what became the United States had its origins in the early Spanish and English colonization of North America and endured as a legal institution until the passage of the Thirteenth Amendment to the United States Constitution in 1865. Although servitude existed in Africa, the status and relationship of African servants to their African masters was very different from that between chattel slaves and their masters. Those held in bondage in Africa were more often considered part of the extended family and maintained a status similar to clansmen. In chattel slavery, those enslaved were the property of the masters and had no legal rights. As property, the chattel could be bought, sold, tortured, and raped at the master's will.

In the African worldwide community, colonization translated to a system of White supremacy. It should be made clear that the singular goal of colonization is to rearrange things to the benefit of the colonizers. When colonization takes place, there are outside forces that enter and rearrange that area, along with all of its resources, to something different than its natural state.

European contact with Africa has always been driven by the desire to transform or rearrange African phenomena into fundamental European constructs in the service of domination and exploitation. Under colonialism Africa's rearrangement was, in most instances, driven by the economic interest of capitalism and the socio-political ideology of White supremacy. There are three methods of colonial reorganization. The first is that colonial reorganization always has to deal with the domination of the physical space. Secondly colonial reorganization requires the managing of the indigenous modes of production. This has been a major problem for Africa as a continent. Managing indigenous modes of production means that the alien integrates its own modes of production into the traditional natural modes of production. Africa was on a path of development that laid out certain notions of family organization, social structures, and political organization, but that was infused into the European notion of political, social, and family functioning. The third method, which perhaps is the most important aspect of colonization, has to do with the reformation or the reforming of the African mind. Once the other two methods have been employed, the ultimate task is to replace the African mind with a European mind, which is done by replacing African indigenous education, religious, and psychological systems.

It is useful to review Hegel's[6] ideas on the dynamics of bondage, which have influenced almost all later theoretical formulations of human oppression. Essentially, Hegel argues that man becomes conscious of himself only through recognition by the other. The frustration of one's desire to be recognized is the source of human struggle and conflict. Hegel asserts that the one who attains recognition without reciprocating becomes the "master." The one who recognizes the other but is not reciprocally recognized becomes the "slave." Hegel further notes that not only does the "master" gain recognition from the "slave," but the "master" also reduces the slave to an instrument of the "master's" will. Basically, Hegel is suggesting that the one whose "humanity" is recognized but does not recognize the "humanity" of the other becomes the master while the one who recognizes the "humanity" of the other while his or her own "humanity" is not recognized becomes the slave. Because the master's humanity is confirmed by other recognition, the idea of self and worth are reflected back to him; and he, thereby, attains "objective truth" of his otherwise subjective sense. When one's humanity is not recognized, the enslaved lacks both objective confirmation and subjective certainty of not just one's self and human worth but of one's self being human. For slavery to work, the adversaries in the dynamic of oppression must adopt two different strategies in the struggle for human recognition. One risks life until recognized and adopts a strategy of conquer or die while the other adopts the strategy of "become a slave" and remain alive and thereby submits to oppression for fear of losing life (death). The master-slave dialectic is further complicated, Hegel suggests, because the master's humanity is limited and compromised by the fact that the master, in totally depending on the slave to fulfill his every need, loses the means of transforming his world and himself. The enslaved, however, according to Hegel, works in the objective world and transforms the world with his labor. By transforming nature, the enslaved also transforms himself. The slave – not the master – is correspondingly self-actualized.

In *Frantz Fanon and the Psychology of Oppression*, Bulhan[7] notes that Hegel's philosophical and intellectual language really obscures the psychological impact of the master-slave formulation. He notes that in a series of lectures on Hegel, Alexander Kojeve[8] reviews Hegel's master-slave dialectic and attempts to articulate the psychological underpinnings of the master-slave relationship. Kojeve notes that self-consciousness differentiates man from animal and that one is self-conscious to the extent that one is conscious of his identity, dignity, and human reality. Animals, he asserts, only have "sentiment" or an unthinking feeling about self. According to Kojeve, desire determines behavior. In terms of human beings, desire determines human action and is bound to reality and the preservation of life. In terms of animals, sentiment, the unthinking feeling associated with living, gives birth to the animal desire to eat or procreate. However, both self-consciousness and sentiment have their origin in desire. Self-consciousness is born from human desire to be recognized by another human being. Human desire goes beyond the instinct of self-preservation. In fact, human desire compels humans to even risk life for recognition.

Kojeve suggests that "it is only by being recognized by another that a human being is really human."[9] Accordingly, a people's humanity is validated because others recognize it; on the other hand, a people's humanity is invalidated because others do not acknowledge them.

One's self-consciousness, as reflected in the search for recognition, entails a perilous struggle between two opposing forces that require recognition from each other. The master/slave dynamic really involves a fight to the death for one's humanity. Manonni[10] believed that the colonial situation was an encounter between two different personality types. He noted in this regard that every culture fosters a typical or particular personality (sum total of beliefs, habits, and propensities) structure that is passed on from one generation to the next. In effect, groups come into contact with other groups carrying a psychological inheritance representing their unique crystallization of individual, family, and group experiences associated with their particular history and environment. Manonni further suggests that the psychological complexes of "inferiority" and "dependency" form two fundamentally and mutually exclusive axes upon which personality and culture develop. Each complex, he believed, was the underlining of a particular "mentality" associated with a particular culture.

The "dependency complex," Manonni argued, engenders socio-economic and technological stagnation and fosters submission and the "need to be ruled" while the "inferiority complex" engenders high development of personality and culture and fosters dominance and the "need to rule." It is not surprising that Manonni asserts that the "dependency complex" is deeply entrenched in the collective consciousness of the African as represented by the Malagasy people. In this regard, he further concludes that the "non-civilized"(i.e., the African man) is totally unfit for a pattern of life absent of complete subjugation, and in fact, needs colonial domination to satisfy his natural dependency complex.

In spite of his Eurocentric bias and intellectual limitations regarding the African, Manonni's insights regarding the European personality and collective unconsciousness may have some utility in furthering the interrogation of the enslavement experience. Manonni suggests that the "inferiority complex" and "misanthropy" characterized the European personality and collective consciousness. He asserts that western (White) man's main driving force and need to rule people who are in distant lands are found in this inferiority complex and misanthropy.

It is the state of non-reciprocal recognition that gives rise to the psychological grounding of the master-slave dialectic. Both Hegel and Manonni posit particular psychological complexes associated with immutable group characteristics or inherent traits that distinguish the master and the slave. Hegel believed that there were inherent qualities (and responsibilities) that allow for the enslavement of particular people. Regarding these "responsibilities and qualities," he asserts, "If a man is a slave, his own will is responsible for his slavery, just as it is his will which is responsible if a people is subjugated." In effect, there is an attribute, quality, or characteristic intrinsic to the enslaved that is responsible for them being enslaved. George A. Kelley[11] argues that Hegel's master-slave dialectic was essentially a metaphor for "inherent traits" (i.e. domination and servitude) found in the human psyche. Hegel's master-slave dialectic is, therefore, a derivative of the basic psychological traits of domination (master) and servitude (slave). The only way to explain, in the struggle for human recognition, why of two protagonists locked in combat, one becomes the master and the other the slave is the master-slave dialectic, which Kelly believes, in fact, actually originated in the "natural inequalities" and "internal imbalances" found in their psychological make-ups. While Hegel's and Manonni's insights can and have been debated ad nauseam, the question remains as to what or how "slavery" and "mastery" are related to psychology or to a psychological understanding of human functioning and relationships.

In *Black Skins White Masks*, Frantz Fanon summarizes Hegel's master-slave dialectic and attempts to use Hegel's paradigm to analyze the relationship between contemporary White and Black people. In formulating his critical analyses of oppression and decolonization, Fanon rightfully notes that colonialism was simply another stage or form of slavery. The colonizer-colonized and the master-slave relationship are identical. Africa's colonization and diaspora chattel enslavement are the unaddressed twin evils infecting the modern world order. Chattel slavery had a destructive psychological impact on diasporic Africans, and colonialism had a similar destructive psychological impact on continental Africans. They, in tandem, were the dehumanizing instruments of the morphing and/or destruction of African ideas and human functioning.

Probably because he was a member of the "wretched of the earth," Frantz Fanon is at his best in unraveling the psychology of the oppressed. Unlike Hegel or Manonni, Fanon surgically points out that the problem of oppression is a problem of violence. Fanon helps us to see that while oppression requires the fear of physical death, the fear is created via the exercise and threat of violence. As an intellectual and psychological theorist, Fanon offered a deeper analysis of the question of violence. Violence, as an integral part of the enslavement process, is so pervasive and structured that it is often viewed as the natural order of life. Fanon makes the point that there are forms of violence that are destructive to the spirit of African people. He noted, for instance, that there is a form of violence that is simply raw vulgar violence. It is simply brute force and physical coercion (i.e. when slaves are physically beaten, brutalized, and tortured, etc.) That is what Fanon called raw, vulgar, violence, coercion, and physical harm.

Fanon also wrote about and talked about "historical violence." Historical violence, he pointed out, consists of the long-term harm that occurs when people are subjected to destruction, plundering, vandalizing, and false systems of pacification. The many examples of colonial or military occupation-pacification programs that result in extermination rather than pacification are strong examples of Fanon's historical violence. The most intriguing form of violence that Fanon identifies is called "violence beyond violence." In terms of "violence beyond violence," Fanon states that this form of violence is the invisible destructive force that is always at work and that expresses itself as an alien form of universal values and dominant norms. In effect, he is saying that when Europe positioned itself as the only universal human system of values and norms, that became "violence beyond violence." Consequently, Europe is seen as the universal standard or example of humanity. However, when African people accept a system of values and norms as universal which removes the African from the stage of human history, this results in a distortion of the African psyche that is devastating. This insidious corruptive element is an almost irreversible aspect of "violence beyond violence" that one is not able to see or hear. Fanon observed that the categorical denial of the integrity of African historical contributions to humanity is the first charge of the violence beyond violence.

Following Hegel's assertion, many European scholars believe that it is necessary to remove Africans from Egypt and Egypt from Africa because the historical contributions of African people to humanity must be destroyed in order to justify the idea that Africans have no humanity. As emblematic of this intellectual falsification, Hegel asserted in a most authoritative and emphatic way that

> At this point we leave Africa, not to mention it again. For it is no historical part of the World; it has no movement or development to exhibit. Historical movements in it—that is in its northern part—belong to the Asiatic or European World. Carthage displayed there an important transitionary phase of civilization; but as a Phoenician colony, it belongs to Asia. Egypt will be considered in reference to the passage of the human mind from its Eastern to its Western phase, but it does not belong to the African Spirit. What we properly understand by Africa, is the Unhistorical, Undeveloped Spirit, still involved in the conditions of mere nature, and which had to be presented here only as on the threshold of the World's History.[12]

This type of "violence beyond violence" is a destructive force created beyond belief and comprehension. "Violence beyond violence" is a compelling and dangerously frightening phenomenon. The very physical survival of our ancestors depended upon their acceptance of the pretense of white supremacy. The defining of

African people and the distortion of everything pertaining to Africa is an example of "violence beyond violence" or what some scholars[13] call Holy Violence, which helps explain Africa's destabilization and African peoples' dehumanization.

It is fundamental that we think deeply about things African. If we do not ever challenge the cultural ground we stand on and the intellectual categories or categorical conceptualizations we utilize, then we will simply continue the process of being victims of "violence beyond violence" and never knowing that we are victims. We do not see the destruction of Rosewood, a historical Black township, as happening to us. We do not see a hundred years of African American lynching as happening to us. We do not see the genocidal Biafran war as happening to us. We don't see the bombing of Tulsa, Oklahoma as happening to us. We do not see the destruction of ancient shrines and historical texts in Mali as happening to us. We do not see the economically motivated destruction of urban Black America as happening to us. We do not see the Hutus and Tutsi Rwandan genocide as happening to us. This acidic erosion of African consciousness is "violence beyond violence." We cannot fathom what is happening anywhere in the African world as happening to us because the psychology of "violence beyond violence" is so subtle that we feel blessed that we escaped, that we got away, that we are still alive, that we are not like the rest of them "niggas," that we are not African.

The oppressed or enslaved live in a world where their physical, and most importantly, their psychological space, is curtailed, intruded upon, and/or denied. Bulhan[14] rightfully observes that life and living are inconceivable without agency over one's space, time, energy, mobility, bonding, and identity. These six dimensions define, determine, and substantiate the human psyche in the form of consciousness and identity. It is through human consciousness and identity that we are even aware that we inhabit time and space or that our energy and mobility have utility and that our relationship (and recognition) with others is fulfilling, nurturing, and inspiring. It is consciousness and identity that give us a sense of self and the awareness of all the possibilities of living. What is not so clear is that the meaning of being human is itself, informed and experienced as coherent and comprehensive through these same six dimensions.

Chattel slavery, however, involves outright ownership of the enslaved by a master. More importantly chattel slavery required making the enslaved human being a movable piece of property—equivalent to a goat, cow, or pig. Chattel slavery, in effect, dehumanized the African human being. No other form of servitude, serfdom, slavery, or indentured labor defined human laborers as less than human. In effect, African consciousness and identity were shattered by an all-pervasive domination of the ancestors' space, time, energy, mobility, bonding, and identity. In dominating these primary dimensions of the psyche, the enslavement and colonial experience created fissures and cracks in the African consciousness and identity. In this sense, chattel slavery is a uniquely American experience whose psychological destruction is only matched by European colonialism.

There is little in recorded human history that compares with the sheer horror of the European psychological assault on Africa and African people. The 300 years of the Trans-Atlantic Slave Trade amounted to a massive unparalleled system of death and destruction beyond human comprehension and convention. The notorious Middle Passage destroyed the lives of (40 to 100 million)[15] innocent human beings. The dehumanizing derailment of Africa's development by colonialism matches that of slavery and is equally unmatched in human history.

---

1   In the field of Black Psychology, as being developed in the United States, the terms Black Psychology, African-centered Psychology, African Centered Psychology, and Pan African (Black) Psychology are often used interchangeably. Throughout this manuscript, that same convention will be followed.

2   From Gaines, A. D. (Ed.). (1992, p.5). *Ethnopsychiatry: The Cultural Construction of Professional and Folk Psychiatries.*

[3] From Khatib, S., McGee. S, Nobles, W., & Akbar, N. (1975). "Voodoo or I.Q.: An introduction to African Psychology," *Journal of Black Psychology,* 1 (2), 1-20.

[4] See Nobles, W. (1972). "African Philosophy: Foundations for Black Psychology." In R. Jones (Ed.), *Black Psychology* (pp. 18-32).This critical shift was further supported in Khatib, McGee, Nobles, & Akbar (1975); King, L., Nobles, W., and Dixon, V. (1976). *African Philosophy: Assumptions and Paradigms for Research on Black People*; see pp. 18-32; and Gaines, A. D. (Ed.). (1992). *Ethnopsychiatry: The Cultural Construction of Professional and Folk Psychiatries*; Nobles, W. (1997). "To Be African or Not To Be: The Question of Identity or Authenticity – Some preliminary Thoughts." In W. Nobles. *Seeking the Sakhu: Foundational Writings for an African Psychology,* (pp. 317-340).

[5] The reader is welcome to review the following writings as reflective of this tradition: Nobles, W. (2006) "African Root and American Fruit: The Black Family." In *Seeking the Sakhu: Foundational Writings for an African Psychology* (pp. 131-144); Nobles, W. (1994). "Implementing Our International Agenda: Step 1," *Psychological Discourse,* 25, pp. 4-5; King, L., Dixon, V., and Nobles, W. (Eds.) (1976). *African Philosophy: Assumptions and Paradigms for Research on Black Persons*; Semaj, L. (1981). "The Black Self: Identity and Models for Psychological Liberation," *Western Journal of Black Studies,* 5(3), pp. 158-171; Akbar, N. (1984). "Afrocentric Social Science for Human liberation," *Journal of Black Studies,* 4, pp. 395-414; Hilliard, A. (1986). "Pedagogy in Ancient Kemet." In M. Karenga & J. H. Carruthers (Eds.) *Kemet and the African Worldview,* (pp. 131-150); Nobles, W. (1986a). *African Psychology: Toward its Reclamation, Reascension and Revitalization*; Nobles, W. (1986b). "Ancient Egyptian Thought and the Renaissance of African (Black) Psychology." In M. Karenga & J. H. Carruthers (Eds.) *Kemet and the African Worldview,* (pp. 100-118); Myers, L. (1988). *Understanding an Afrocentric Worldview*; Parham, T.A. (1989). "Cycles of Psychological Nigrescence," *The Counseling Psychologist,* 17(2), pp. 187-226; Akbar, N. (1990). "African American Consciousness and Kemet: Spirituality, Symbolism and Duality." In M. Karenga (Ed.) *Reconstructing Kemetic Culture: Papers, Perspectives, Projects* (pp. 99-114); Kambon, K. (1992). *The African Personality in America: An African-centered Framework*; Wilson, A. (1993).*The Falsification of Afrikan Consciousness: Eurocentric History, Psychiatry and the Politics of White Supremacy*; Grills, C. & Rowe, D. (1998). "African Traditional Medicine: Implications for African Centered Approaches to Healing." In In R. Jones (Ed.), *African Mental Health*; Nobles, W. (1997). "To Be African or Not to Be: The Question of Identity or Authenticity – Some preliminary Thoughts." In R. Jones (Ed.), *African American Identity Development: Theory, Research and Intervention* (pp. 185-206).

[6] From Hegel, G. (1966, pp. 229-240). *The Phenomenology of the Mind.*

[7] From Bulhan, H. (1966, pp. 102-107). *Frantz Fanon and the Psychology of Oppression.*

[8] From Kojève, A. (1969, p. 9). *Introduction to the Reading of Hegel.*

[9] From Kojève, p. 25.

[10] From Mannoni, O. (1962, p. 40). *Prospero and Caliban: The Psychology of Colonization.*

[11] From Stewart, J. (1998, pp. 444-469). *The Phenomenology of Spirit Reader: Critical and Interpretive Essays.*

[12] See Hegel, G. (1956, p. 99). Hegel further attempts to justify the lack of African humanity by asserting that "the peculiarly African character is difficult to comprehend, for the very reason that in reference to it, we must quite give up the principle which naturally accompanies all our ideas—the category of Universality." A closer reading of Hegel should help the reader to understand how his thinking shaped much of the future intellectual discussion of the value of African thought and beliefs as belonging to the discourse on universal human understanding.

[13] From Perimbaum, M. (1982, pp.15-29). *Holy Violence: The Revolutionary Thought of Frantz Fanon: An Intellectual Biography.*

[14] From Bulhan, p.124.

[15] Nobles, N., Crawford, J. & Leary, J. (2003, pp. 251-281). "Reparations and Health Care for African Americans: Repairing the Damage from the legacy of Slavery." In R. Winbush (Ed.) *Should America Pay? Slavery and the Raging Debate on Reparations.*

Chapter Two

Memetic Ideation and the Shattering of the African Mind

The psychological effect that European imperialism, in the form of slavery and colonialism, has had on Africa and her people has never been fully addressed and understood. Fueled by an ideology of white supremacy, the rise of European capitalism directly influenced the trade in captured and enslaved Africans. New World plantation colonies grew and prospered using enslaved Africans as a permanent labor force. This free labor had a great impact on the sugar, cotton, tobacco, indigo, and coffee industrial plantations. A lucrative triangular trade[1, 2] was established. Alcohol, firearms, and textiles were shipped from Europe to be traded for captured Africans. These Africans would then be shipped to the Caribbean and the Americas where they would be traded for staples, such as molasses and raw cotton.

Africa lost from 40 to 100 million souls to the illicit trade in human beings. This human derailment was experienced at a personal level as psychological terror and physical torture. Human beings were chained together and then piled on top of each other where they had to lay and sleep in their excrement as well as that of the persons crowded next to them for weeks on end. A vicious cycle of disease[3] ensued as African people huddled together crying, screaming, vomiting, and defecating uncontrollably. Along this human chain of misery, some were dead and some alive; the waft of rotting bodies added to the stench. There was no escape from disease. Life on the plantation simply continued the terror and torture. One can only imagine the state of mental health for those trapped in this living nightmare. Psychologically, panic, anxiety, and hysteria prevailed. Pure rage alternated with a deep collective depression manifesting in mutinies, on-board rebellions, and constant and continuous slave revolts. Africa's human capital of intellect, insight, and imagination was depleted and/or deformed at the very moment in history when humanity was moving into a new age.

The colonization of continental Africa resulted in similar psychological terror and torture. The avaricious and arbitrary dissection and shattering of Africa resulted in seemingly endless conflicts due to torn loyalties and/or unhealthy ethnic pluralities with different tribes vying for Western-based governmental power[4]. The legacy of colonization has become Africa's untreated cancer in the guise of development.

The Berlin Conference of 1885[5], where the European powers of Belgium, Italy, Great Britain, Portugal, France, Germany, and Holland met to divide Africa and its peoples into "properties" of each of the imperial nations, was actually the culmination of Europe's assault on Africa. In so doing, the conference in Berlin determined the fate and future of Africa, both continental and Diasporic, and has led to endless cycles of African dysfunction and human misery.

In the Democratic Republic of the Congo (formerly known as the Belgian Congo), for example, King Leopold II's savagery, under the cloak of development, has been inestimable. Forcing Africans to work the valuable rubber resource, his torture was applied to men, women, and children alike with amputations, floggings, and the burning of villages and the wholesale killing of Africans. The endless cycle of African death and dysfunction in the name of so-called development continues up to the present day with conflicts in Liberia, Rwanda, Sierra Leone, and Cote d'Ivoire spurned on by Western industrial monopolies and/or the continuation of cycles of power between those who benefitted from the support of the provincial government during colonial times and those who did not. Another consequence of colonization is the imbalance of power between African transformational industry and Western industrial monopolies, which produce the final goods that are sold in the rich markets of the developed world without sharing the wealth with Africa.

The shattering of Africa has made African unity and solvency a requisite component of all "developmental initiatives." In speaking to the new generation of African leaders, Julius Nyere admonished them to:

> *"...work for unity with firm convictions that without unity there is no future for Africa. That is, of course, if we still want to have a place in the sun. I reject the glorification of the*

*nation-state, which we have inherited from colonialism, and
the artificial nations we are trying to forge from that inheritance. Unity will not make us rich, but it can make it difficult
for Africa and African people to be disregarded and humiliated. And it will, therefore, increase the effectiveness of the
decisions we make and try to implement for our development.*"[6]

While colonialism has left most African countries in a situation
of great economic weakness and dependence, the real legacy
of colonialism and chattel slavery is the unspoken harm resulting
from an invisible psychological terrorism in the form of educating
generations of Africans, both continental and Diasporic, to become
alienated from their own essential worth addicted to anything non-
African, especially White thought, behaviors, and beliefs and a
willingness to exchange or even sacrifice Africa's development for
access to White privilege and power.

Critical to understanding the clash of culture and consciousness is the idea of memes and memetic ideation and their role in
Europe's psychological domination of Africa's mind. The clash is
centered on the meaning of being human and the question of human relations, both of which can be illuminated by the utilization of
"memetic analyses." In *The Evolution of Evolutionability*, Richard
Dawkins[7] defines "memes" as a unit of cultural inheritance that is
naturally selected by virtue of its phenotypic consequence on the
particular culture's survival and replication in the cultural environment. The meme itself is defined as a unit of information residing
in the brain. Its phenotypic effects are the external consequences
of the memetic information. Words, skills, behaviors, etc., he suggests, are the outward and visible manifestations of the memes
within the brain, which are transmitted between individuals via the
sense organs. Memes use their possessor's communication and
imitation skills in order to replicate themselves and by influencing
the world in which their possessor dwells, increase their chances
of survival. It can, however, be argued that memes are more than
just units of information residing in the brain.

In furthering Dawkins' ideas, memes could also be thought of as contagious symbiotic reproductive sensoria-information structures and patterns, including all of the senses that influence human knowing and awareness. In doing so, the sensoria-information structure/patterns can alter behavior and propagate patterns of behavior to be consistent with the sensoria-information structures/patterns. Expanding on the idea of memes, sensoria-information structures/patterns, in the form of symbols, sounds, touch, and/or movement, are capable of being perceived by any of the senses and alter behavior in a way that is consistent with and propagates the sensoria. Sensoria-information structures/patterns, like memes, should be thought of as orienting ideas, which act like a self-replicating nexus for the propagation and legitimation of behavioral dispositions and functioning. Accordingly, sensoria-information structures/patterns can be thought of as units of cultural discourse or orienting ideas, which in influencing human consciousness direct and determine meaning for the cultural agents who carry the meme. In effect, memes are ideas and information, which are the substance of behavior. Fundamentally or foundationally memes serve as "epistemic memetic nodes," which shape and support a particular aesthetic, moral code, and behavioral norms.

As sensorial information structures, "memes" need to be able to "pass on" from one generation to the next while preserving their core content or meaning and capacity to preserve the altered behavior. Many believe that imitation is one of the most obvious methods by which cultural information spreads. It is thought that by observing another's actions, one can learn (via imitation) to do what others do or be as they are. Through education and/or indoctrination, memetic information is shrouded with the intentionality of grasping consciously or unconsciously a subject or acquiring certain information, ideas, values, beliefs, and behaviors that are valuable for future life performance and the promotion of one's welfare and well-being.

Memory, like consciousness, is generally thought of as something that individuals have going on "inside" their heads. In gener-

al, memory is thought of as having several referential schemas, all
of which are located in the mind. The conventional notion of both
memory and consciousness being stored or located within the
mind of each individual is somewhat problematic. Within western
thought, Emile Durkeim's notion of a "collective consciousness"[8]
is closer to an African understanding of memory. Durkeim suggests that rather than individually based memory, the recollection
of a shared past, retained by a group who experienced a common past, could be defined as "collective memory." There remain,
however, epistemological limitations with this notion of collective
memory.

The process by which sensorial-information structures symbiotically infect the mind or consciousness so as to reinforce and/
or propagate the sensorial is called "memetic ideation." Thus,
one can classify types of consciousness or mentalities (e.g. slave
mentality, Black consciousness, Franco/Anglophone, etc.) by the
defining nature of the memetic cluster fundamental to its character. Through these processes, memetic information is shrouded
with the intentionality of grasping a subject or acquiring certain
information, ideas, values, beliefs, and behaviors that are valuable
for future life performance – especially that information related to
the promotion of one's welfare and well-being. However, education can be dangerous if it involves the transmission of pieces of
information that serve as epistemic memetic nodes. An example of
a memetic node is the idea that individual freedom has no boundaries or that the physical life is all that exists.

Memes or sensoria-information structures can be in the form of
ideas, symbols, images, feelings, words, customs, sounds, practices, or any other knowable and perceptible item or substance.
Religion, political dogma, social philosophy or movements, aesthetics and artistic styles, traditions, customs, and every component of culture (behaviors, ideas, attitudes, values, habits, beliefs,
language, rituals, ceremonies, and practices) co-evolve and serve
in symbiotic relationships as a meme-complex. The integrative
complex of ideas, symbols, images, feelings, words, customs, attitudes, values, habits, beliefs, language, rituals, ceremonies, prac-

tices sounds, movement, religious worship, political dogma, social philosophy, aesthetics, artistic styles, traditions, and customs can all be seen as "memetic ideations."

A memetic analysis of the age of feudalism in Europe will identify the impact of the "memetic ideation" of royalty and aristocracy, which were rooted in ancient Greco-Roman thought. The term aristocracy is derived from the Greek "aristokratia," meaning "rule of the best." The "memetic ideation" of "the best" ruling evolved in ancient Greece where, in contrast to a monarchy, a council of prominent citizens ruled. Privileged by birth and wealth as "memetic ideations," this group of prominent citizens was allowed to form an elite aristocratic class.

In medieval Europe, aristocratic rule was further embedded in the system of feudalism where lords (aristocrats) controlled the lands of the realm. It is interesting to note that the etymology of the word, lord, is found in the old English word, *"hlaford"* or *"hlaf-weard,"* meaning "bread keeper" or "load-ward," which reflects the idea that some people were literally the determiners of life and death by their ability to survive at a very basic level by controlling the availability of food. The concept of "vassal" was also a critical component of feudalism. The etymology of vassal comes from the Celtic word *"gwas,"* meaning boy and is associated with a Latinized form *"vassus."* The vassals were gangs of young men who voluntarily subjected themselves to the authority and rulership of a leader (the best) whose distributions of loot was where the vassals would be fed, clothed, and armed. Under the European system of feudalism, a "memetic ideation," land or revenue producing property (fief) was granted by a lord in return for a pledge of allegiance and loyalty. The "fief" idea could be anything of value (e.g., an office, title, right to exploitation, and/or anything that produced revenue) and as a "memetic ideation," would affect (or "infect") the consciousness and thus alter the behavior of both the lord and peasant.

France, under the *Ancien Régime* (the monarchy before the French Revolution), embraced a set of memetic ideas, which divided society into three estates: the *First Estate* or clergy; the *Sec-*

ond Estate or nobility; and the *Third Estate* or commoners. Parenthetically, it should be noted that the Seven-Year War (1756-1763),
a conflict involving all of the major European powers, was in fact a
conflict amongst the various aristocracies to decide dominance (a
memetic idea) over the exploitation (a memetic idea) of the world's
revenue producing assets. Essentially, out of the European mind
came a social system (memetic cluster) comprised of lords (aristocrats), vassals, and peasants (the poor, exploited, and enslaved).

The area of memes and memetic analyses may have some
utility in understanding the impact of slavery. Memetics, in this
regard, will be utilized to reframe our understanding of the psychological impact of the Trans-Atlantic Slave Trade. The terminology
of memetics allows us to further excavate the process of enslavement and to isolate its lingering effects as components or precise
features of psychic terror as evidenced in the shattering of African
consciousness and fractured Black identity. As noted the "memetic
infection" or antagonistic sensoria-information structure would be
any contagious alien information pattern that replicates by symbiotically infecting human minds and altering behavior and thereby
causing the alien meme to propagate the pattern.

Memetic infection would, in fact, suggest that the contagious
information pattern that replicated itself via infecting the minds of
the enslaved Africans was an identifiable complex of ideas and
experiences that supported the belief that the African was "chattel"
and void of human value and worth. Supported by this memetic
infection, the only behaviors and beliefs allowable were those
representing dependency, inferiority, passivity, servility, meek-
ness, obedience, and fearfulness. The fundamental question for
the memetic analysis of the trade in enslaved Africans is to re-
interrogate the American slavery experience as a meme-complex.
Functionally, memes are any contagious information pattern in
the form of symbols, sounds, and/or movement that is capable of
being perceived by any of the senses and replicated by symbiotically entering the human being's "mind" and thus altering behavior
in a way that propagates itself. Simplistically, therefore, a meme
is an orienting idea, which acts like a self-replicating nexus for the

propagation and legitimation of behavioral dispositions. "Contagious information pattern" can be summarized as or referred to as an orienting idea. Therefore, a meme can be thought of as a unit of cultural discourse that in influencing human consciousness directs and determines meaning for the cultural agents who carry the meme.

Memes should be thought of as any of the sensorial that serve to guide, direct, and define or give meaning to behavior.[9] As alienating sensorial information structures, "memetic infections" can transmit to the next generation their core content or meaning and capacity to preserve the altered behavior. The more fundamental the orienting idea embedded in the sensorial information structure, the more it serves as a process or germ and in effect, functions to influence the very process of knowing itself. These fundamental or foundational memes, in turn, serve as "epistemic memetic nodes," which shape and support a particular aesthetic, moral code, and set of human relations.

From the Middle Ages up to the Age of Enlightenment and Discovery, Europe's presence in the world can be defined as the Age of Slaveocracy and/or dehumanization. The memetic ideations supported by European slaveocracy are aristocracy, class privilege, fief (revenue producing property), inherited role status (hierarchies), elitism, subjugation, life-long slavery, ideological conflict, genetic inferiority, apostolic authority, exaltation of Christ and Christianity, ownership of land and people, divine sanction, and general "whiteness" (viewed as sacred, superior, and powerful). As mentioned above, in serving as "epistemic memetic nodes," these ideas also serve to define and influence issues from the aesthetic to the contours and context of human relations. This was the "memetic ideation" system to which Africans were introduced as victims of enslavement and colonization.

The lingering psychological effects of the enslavement experience and the specific psychological processes that distorted and corrupted Black identity and African consciousness should be considered a "memetic infection." In relation to consciousness, sensoria are not only or exclusively located or experienced in the mind nor are they the aggregate collection of individual recollections. It is, however, a fuller appreciation of the sensorial content of consciousness that can better illuminate our understanding of the meme(ry) of being enslaved.

---

[1] From Emmer, P. (1998).The Dutch in the Atlantic Economy, 1580–1880: Trade, Slavery and Emancipation.

[2] From Morgan, K. (1993, pp. 64-77). *Bristol and the Atlantic Trade in the Eighteenth Century.*

[3] Nobles, N., Crawford, J. & Leary, J. (2003, pp. 251-281). "Reparations and Health Care for African Americans: Repairing the Damage from the legacy of Slavery." In R. Winbush (Ed.) *Should America Pay? Slavery and the Raging Debate on Reparations.*

[4] Pakenham, T. (1991).The Scramble for Africa: *White Man's Conquest of the Dark Continent from 1876 to 1912;* Mommsen, W., Forster, S., & Robinson, R. (1989). *Bismarck, Europe, and Africa: The Berlin Africa Conference 1884–1885 and the Onset of Partition.*

[5] See Rothschild, A. (1998). *King Leopold's Ghost.*

[6] Shivji, I. (2009) "Nyerere's Nationalist Legacy," *Pambazuka News*, p. 460.

[7] Dawkins, R. (1989). "The Evolution of Evolutionability." In E. C. Langton (Ed.) *Artificial Life.*

[8] The idea of collective conscious or collective conscience was introduced by the French sociologist Émile Durkheim in his *Division of Labour in Society* in 1893.

[9] Erlyn, P. & Rowe, D. (2010) "Educating African-centered psychologists: Towards a comprehensive paradigm," *Journal of Pan-African Studies*, 3(8), pp. 5-23.

Chapter Three

Hispaniola's Memetic Infection: A Reinterrogation of the Enslavement Experience

To understand the contemporary problems of color and class in Haiti, one has first to understand the Haitian mind as infected by Spain and France and their European "memetic ideation." Isabella and Ferdinand's reign heralded a golden age and marked the beginning of Spain's modern history. The marriage of the royal teenaged cousins, Ferdinand of Aragon (17 years old) and Isabella of Castile (18 years old), in 1469 signaled the beginning of Spain's influence as a world power.[1] This scenario would not have occurred had it not been for the influence of the Catholic Church. In fact, Spain and Portugal added the influence of "the *Papacy*" (as a memetic idea) to the conceptual atmosphere of aristocracy, vassals, and peasantry. The influence of Catholicism can be seen in the 14th- century directives from various popes. In 1452, Pope Nicholas V, for example, issued the papal bull, *Dum Diversas*, which authorized and "ushered in the West African slave trade." The *Dumas Diversas* states:

> We grant you [Kings of Spain and Portugal] by these present documents, with our Apostolic Authority, full and free permission to invade, search out, capture, and subjugate the Saracens and pagans and any other unbelievers and enemies of Christ wherever they may be, as well as their kingdoms, duchies, counties, principalities, and other property [...] and to reduce their persons into perpetual slavery.[2]

The "memetic ideation" stemming from the *Dumas Diversas Papal Bull* was the idea of "apostolic authority," "subjugation," "punished class," and "perpetual slavery." The papal bull specifically gave Portugal the right to reduce any "Saracens, pagans, and any other unbelievers" to hereditary slavery. The approval of slavery under these conditions was reaffirmed and extended in Pope Nicholas V's *Romanovs Pontific Bull* of 1455. The *Dumas Diversas* and *Rominanus Pontific* essentially planted the idea that God wanted the Saracens (those recognized as coming from the Fatimid Empire of North Africa, who was seen as "not from Sarah,"[3] cf., Book of Genesis[4]), who were the enemies of Christ and as appropriate to their constitution or nature, to be made perpetual slaves. These papal bulls crafted a memetic ideation which coupled apostolic authority and subjugation (as condoned by God) in the form of perpetual destruction, misery, and slavery.

In 1456, Pope Calixtus III reiterated the bull with *Etsi Cuncti*, which was renewed by Pope Sixtus IV in 1481. The concept (or memetic idea) of the consignment of exclusive spheres of influence to certain nation states was extended to the Americas in 1493 by Pope Alexander VI with *Inter Caetera*, which formally approved the division of the unexplored world between Spain and Portugal. The language of the *Inter Caetera* while obtuse is representative of the time and informative as to the memetic ideation that governed the imperial world domination of Spain and Portugal and the onslaught of the Trans-Atlantic Slave Trade. The "memetic ideation" embedded in this document was that (1) Christ must be exalted above all else and Christianity spread everywhere (lines 6, 38-45), (2) any act in the service of this Divine mission was honoring God (line 16), and (3) state or theocratic sanctioned ownership of lands and their peoples was consistent with divine will (lines 46-54). The bull explicitly stated that as a reward for this divine work, you, your heirs, and successors would be rewarded with everything belonging to the enemies of Christ.[5]

The Treaty of Tordesillas, which Spain and Portugal signed in 1494, moved the line of division westward and allowed Portugal to claim Brazil. With the sanction and directive of religious papacy, Spain and Portugal set out to explore and exploit the peoples and resources of the new world. Towards the end of the 15th century, Portuguese mariners opened a route around Africa to the East. The Castilians established colonies in the Azores and in the Canary Islands, which were assigned to Spain by papal decree.

Ferdinand and Isabella's "Holy War" (1483-1492) to subjugate Granada resumed the re-conquest and captured Granada, earning them the title of Catholic Kings from Pope Alexander VI. The surrender and conquest of Granada on January 2, 1492, allowed the Catholic Kings to direct their attention to world domination. Queen Isabella supported Christopher Columbus in his plan to reach the Indies by sailing west. Columbus' conditions were that he was made "Admiral of the Seas," governorship for him and his descendants of lands to be discovered, and ten percent of all profits. Clearly, The Catholic Kings' conquest of the "New World" was driven by greed, personal and regency profit, and papal decree to dominate and exploit those not of the Catholic faith.

Columbus' first expedition to the supposed Indies actually landed in the Bahamas on October 12, 1492. He landed on the island of Guanahani and named it San Salvador. He then continued onto Cuba, which he named Juana. He finished this journey on the island of Santo Domingo, calling it La Española.

Almost a year to the day later, when Columbus came back from Spain on his second voyage, he arrived (November 27, 1493) hoping to see a bustling village. However, when he landed, he found the corpses of his men on the beach and discovered that La Navidad had been destroyed. He was told by the Tainos that the settlers had mistreated the natives, and as retaliation all of the invading Spaniards were killed.

In 1496, Columbus negotiated with a powerful native woman named Anacaona (1464–c.1504)[6] for a tribute of food and cotton to be paid by her people, the Tainos, to the Spanish invaders. Referred to as the Golden Flower, Anacaona was a Taíno *cacique* (chief) and was celebrated as a composer of ballads and narrative poems called *areítos*. She became chief of Jaragua after her brother's death. Her husband Caonabo, who was suspected of having organized the attack on La Navidad, was captured by Alonso de Ojeda and shipped to Spain. Emblematic of Spanish savagery, upon trapping Anacoana and her regional chieftains, the Spanish Governor Nicolás de Ovando executed all 84 of the regional chiefs and offered the reigning ruler of the Taíno and composer of beautiful ballads, Anacaona, clemency if she would submit to their sexual exploitation and serve as a concubine to the Spanish conquerors. Anacoana, chief of the Jaragua, chose death rather than dishonor her people. Anacaona, at twenty-nine years old, was executed by hanging.

On this second voyage, Columbus brought 1,500 colonists with him and established the first European colony in the New World. On this trip, he decided to build a settlement farther east in the present day Dominican Republic and named it *La Isabella*, after Queen Isabella. He immediately initiated the first transatlantic slave voyage with a shipment of several hundred Taíno people sent from Hispaniola to Spain. In 1496, the town of *Nueva Isabella* was founded later to be destroyed by a hurricane. Over a three-year period from 1493 to 1496, the Taíno population of the island was literally decimated by the harsh treatment and disease brought by the Spaniards.

Concerned that Spain ensure control of the natives in the newly conquered Americas, the "Reyes Católicos," Ferdinand and Isabella, consulted theologians and jurists for religious and legal justification of Spain's conquests. The treatment[7] of the Native Americans was at first rationalized on the grounds that they were cannibals. Any means of subjugation were acceptable. In 1500, the king and queen again sought advice, and the Native Americans were declared to be "free vassals."[8]

In 1501, the Spaniards began the systematic kidnapping of Africans, believing them to be more capable of performing physical labor. In 1508, Ferdinand II of Aragon, a Catholic, officially established Spain's African slave trade and two years later, officially started the systematic transportation of Africans to the New World with the authorization of a shipment of 50 enslaved Africans to be sent to Santo Domingo.

New discoveries and conquests came in quick succession. Vasco Nunez de Balboa reached the Pacific in 1513, and the survivors of Ferdinand Magellan's expedition completed the circumnavigation of the globe in 1522. In 1519 the conquistador Hernando Cortes subdued the Aztecs in Mexico with a handful of followers, and between 1531 and 1533, Francisco Pizzaro overthrew the empire of the Incas and established Spanish dominion over Peru.

About 30 years after the killing of Queen Anacoana and the destruction of the last Taino Kingdom by Spain (circa 1625),

French invaders, pirates, and criminals landed on the island of Tortuga and named the colony on the Northwestern Hispaniola Saint Domingue after the Dominican friars. In 1625 the French established the city of "Port-de-Paix," and five years later King Louis XIV (1638-1715) of France authorized the kidnapping and transport of Africans to Saint Domingue.

Colonialism, Slavery and the Morphing of African Ideas and Being

Louis XIV wanted to increase his power in the colonies, and one of his more infamous decrees was the *Grande Ordonnance sur les Colonies* (1685)[9], also known as *Code Noir*. The *Code Noir* defined the conditions of slavery in the French colonial empire, restricted the activities of free Negroes, forbade the exercise of any religion other than Roman Catholicism, and ordered all Jews out of France's colonies. In sanctioning slavery, the code did prohibit the separation of families. Additionally, in the colonies, only Roman Catholics could own slaves, and these had to be baptized. At that time in the Caribbean, Jews were mostly active in the Dutch colonies, so their presence was seen as a Dutch influence. Also at that time, the enslaved Africans were the majority of the population of the French Caribbean, and slave revolts were frequent.

The Black Codes were appropriately entitled as they presented a set of regulations that prescribed the rules and responsibilities for both the enslaved Africans and the masters who held them in captivity. The articles were crafted as specific regulations (memetic ideas) concerning slavery and Catholicism. For example, the articles specified that enslaved Africans must be baptized in the Roman Catholic Church (Article 2), the exercise of any religion other than Catholicism was forbidden(Article 3), slave masters must be Roman Catholic (Article 4), all colonial subjects and slaves must observe Catholic holidays regardless of their own faith, and no one must work on Sundays or on holidays (Article 6), slave markets must not be held on Catholic holidays (Article 7), and only Catholic marriages would be recognized (Article 8).

A good amount of attention was given to the consequence of sexual relations with the enslaved. The *Code Noir* established (memetic ideas) that married free men would be fined for having children with their slave concubines. If the man himself is the master of the slave concubine, the slave and child will be removed from his ownership. If the man was not married, he should then marry the slave concubine thus freeing her and the child from slavery (Article 9). The codes also stipulated that weddings between slaves were to be carried out only with their masters' permission (Article 10) and that the enslaved could not be married without their own consent (Article 11). The codes also determined the Africans' status even before they were born—another memetic idea. The codes stated, in this regard, that children born between married slaves would be slaves, belonging to the female slave's master (Article 12), and that children from the union of a male slave and a female free woman are free, while children of a female slave and a free man are slaves (Article 13). Hence the status of the female determined the status of the offspring.

Controlling the treatment, and more so the will and behavior of the enslaved, was also of great concern. In regard to the treatment of the enslaved, the codes stipulated that masters must give food (quantities specified) and clothes to their slaves, even when they are sick or old (Article 22- 27). A master who falsely accused a slave of a crime and had the slave put to death would be fined (Article 40). Masters could, short of torture and mutilation, chain and beat slaves (Article 42), and those masters who killed their slaves would be punished (Article 43). The codes also clarified that the enslaved were, in fact, community property and could not be mortgaged. As property, the sale was to be equally split between the master's inheritors. The proceeds of their sale could also be used as payment of a debt or bankruptcy (Article 44-46, 48-54). Those enslaved who were married (and their prepubescent children) under the same master are not to be sold separately (Article 47). Masters of freed slaves who gave refuge to fugitive slaves would be fined (Article 39). Slaves who were declared to be sole legatees by their masters, named as executors of wills, or served as tutors of the master's children were to be held and considered as freed slaves (Article 56).

Regarding the will and behavior of the enslaved, the codes ensured that they were not allowed to carry weapons except under permission of their masters for hunting purposes (Article 15); a slave who strikes his or her master, his wife, mistress, or children will be executed (Article 33); slaves belonging to different masters may not gather at any time under any circumstance (Article 16). The enslaved were not allowed to sell sugar cane, even with permission of their masters (Article 18), and they were not allowed to sell any other commodity without the permission of their masters (Article 19-21). The enslaved were allowed to testify in legal proceedings but only for information (Article 30-32). Fugitive slaves absent for a month could have their ears cut off and be branded. If they were found to be absent for another month, their hamstrings could be cut and branded again. On the third time they would be executed (Article 38). The codes stipulated that freed slaves are French subjects, even if born elsewhere (Article. 57), and have the same rights as French colonial subjects (Article 59). However, they (freed slaves) must show special respect to their former masters and their family members (Article 58).

The *Code Noir* can be reread as memetic ideations. As memetic documents, the law of Maryland, (Act of 1715, chap. 44, sec. 23,) and a similar one in South Carolina (in 1711) permit the baptism of slaves, but carefully provides that "such baptism shall not be construed to effect the emancipation of any slave." This arose from a contrary apprehension growing out of ancient usages in England, and the opinion of some jurists that Christians could not be lawfully enslaved.

King Louis XIV's *Code Noir* of 1685 is reproduced in memetic form as the Louisiana Slave Penal Codes of 1724, which legalized the following memetic ideas. Slaves can have nothing that does not belong to their masters, in whatever way acquired (Article XXII). Masters will be held responsible for what their slaves have done by their command (Article XXIII). Slaves are forbidden from exercising public functions, from serving as arbitrators or experts, from giving testimony except in default of white people, and from ever serving as witnesses for or against their masters (Article

XXIV). Any slave who shall have struck his master, his mistress, or the husband of his mistress, or their children, so as to produce a bruise or shedding of blood in the face, shall be put to death (Article XXVII). Outrages or acts of violence against free persons committed by slaves shall be punished with severity and even with death if the case requires it (Article XXVIII).

The Enslavement Experience

Almost a hundred years later, the Legislature of Virginia (1831) continues the memetic assault in passing a law by which any free colored person who undertakes to preach or conduct a religious meeting by day or night may be whipped, not exceeding thirty-nine lashes, at the discretion of *any* justice of the peace; and *anyone* may apprehend any such free colored person *without a warrant*. The same penalty, adjudged and executed in the same way, falls on any slave or free colored person who attends such preaching, and any slave who listens to any *white* preacher in the night-time receives the same punishment. The same law prevails in Georgia and Mississippi.[10] A master *may* permit a slave to preach on *his* plantation, to none but *his* slaves.[11]

Unleashed by European memetic clusters (contagious information patterns and ideas), for the next half-century, Europe invaded Africa, kidnapped its men, women, and children without any serious objection from the world powers. France and Spain enslaved Africans in Saint Domingue. The memetic ideation of the *Code Noir* essentially codified the European memetic cluster and created laws, which resulted in a symbiotic infection of human consciousness so as to support behaviors that reinforced and/or propagated "whiteness." Frenchness, as sensate sensoria, had the attributes of sacred, superior, authoritative, accountable, deserving to be obedient to, omnipotent, having the power over life and death, and that civilized, in deed and image, was only equaled to White (French) people.

---

[1] From Liss, P.K. (2004, pp. TBD). *Isabel the Queen: Life and Times;* See Davidson, M. (1997, p. 474). *Columbus then and now: A Life Reexamined.*

[2] The Bull Inter Caetera (Alexander VI), May 4, 1493. Retrieved from http://www.nativeweb.org/pages/legal/indig-inter-caetera.html.

[3] From Hood, R. (1994, p. 117). *Begrimed and Black: Christian Traditions on Blacks and Blackness.*

[4] From *The Holy Bible*, International Version, Genesis, 17:15-23.

[5] From Verzil, J.H.W., Heere, W.P. & Offerhaus, J.P.S. (1997, pp. 230-234, 237). *International Law in Historical Perspective.*

[6] See Danticat, E. (2005). *Anacaona: Golden Flower, Haiti 1490.*

[7] From Wilson, S. (1990). *Hispaniola - Caribbean Chiefdoms in the Age of Columbus.*

[8] In 1501, the Spaniards began the systematic kidnapping of Africans, believing them to be more capable of performing physical labor. What is more likely to be true is that the genocidal treatment of the Arawak people required the securing of African people as another free labor force.

[9] Code Noir (The Black Code): Collection of Edicts, Statements and Judgments Concerning the Negro Slaves of America (1685) http://www.axl.cefan.ulaval.ca/amsudant/guyanefr1685.htm.

[10] From Goodell, W. (1853). *The American Slave Code in Theory and Practice: Its Distinctive Features Shown by Its Statutes, Judicial Decisions, and Illustrative Facts.*

[11] See Child, L. (1833, p. 67). *Appeal in Favor of That Class of Americans Called Africans.*

Chapter Four

Haiti's Irritated Genie, Phantom of Liberty and Legacy of Memes: Revisiting the Alligator Swamp

During centuries of interaction between Europeans and Africans, African ideations (ideas and beliefs), for the most part, have gone unexamined. Few acknowledge that while undergoing extreme assault and derailment, the African spirit never accepted the slaughter, kidnapping, and enslavement of her children. Intermingling with the Arawak people, the assaulted Africans of then Saint Domingue were primarily Dahomians, Igbo, Nago, Hausa, Aja, Ewe, and Fon from West Africa (currently, Benin, Togo, and Nigeria) and BaKongo and Mandingo from Central Africa (currently, Angola and Kongo). Jean-Bertrand Aristide, former president of Haiti, noted in this regard that the BaNtu philosophy of UbuNtu gave the captive Africans of Saint Domingue "an unmatched strength to resist slavery."[1] It was, in fact, this African philosophical thread that gave the captive Africans certainty in the belief that all people were naturally possessed with dignity and that no one should treat anyone like an animal. It was this same philosophical or more accurately spiritual system that nurtured the seed of resistance and revolution. The revolt and raiding of self-liberated Africans who conducted continuous raids against the plantations were a major concern for the colonial administrators[2].

From the early 1500s up to and beyond the Haitian revolution, Africans and Indians consistently struggled against European oppression and domination. While often overlooked, the evidence of African resistance to dehumanization and captivity throughout the diaspora is documented by the sheer number of revolts. A review of major resistance efforts reads almost like an annual calendar: Gloucester County Revolt, Virginia (1663) ; Slave revolt, New York (1712); Slave conspiracy in Norfolk and Princess Anne counties, Virginia (1730); Stono Rebellion, South Carolina (1739); Massachusetts Slaves' Petition to Legislature for Freedom (1773); Haitian Revolution (1791); Gabriel Prosser in Richmond, Virginia (1800); Charles Deslondes, Revolt New Orleans (1811), the largest slave revolt in the United States[3], Denmark Vesey in Charleston, South Carolina. (1822), Race riot, Cincinnati, Ohio (1829),

Nat Turner Revolt, Southampton County, Virginia (1831), and Amistad Mutiny led by Joseph Cinque (1839).[4]

The establishment of the Slave Codes, in fact, serves as a direct response to the need to control African resistance. African resistance caused the enactment of legal suppression in the form of Black Codes: Barbados Slave Act (1661); Jamaica Slave Act (1664); Barbados Slave Act Amended (1676); Act of the Governing of Negroes, Barbados (1688); South Carolina Slave Act (1691); Jamaica Slave Act (1696); South Carolina Slave Act (1696); Antigua Slave Act (1697); "An act declaring the Negro, Mulatto, and Indian slaves within this dominion (Virginia), to be real estate" (1705); Act for the Better Ordering and Governing of Negroes and Slaves (1712); The "Black Code" of Louisiana (1724); Thomas Jefferson: A Bill Concerning Slaves (1779); Black Laws of Ohio (1804); Washington's Black Code (1808); Slave Codes of the State of Georgia (1848); Louisiana Black Codes: An act relative to apprentices and indentured servants (1865); and Black Codes of Mississippi (1865).

In this same vein, Africans in Saint Domingue fought against their enslavement and sought to avenge the killing of their family, clan, and kinsmen. Colonial administration records document the haunting memory of maroon chief Polydor's slave revolt (one of many) and the difficulty in capturing him in 1734.[5] In 1785 the colonial administrators of both Spanish and French colonies signed a treaty with the maroon community living in the frontier region of Bahoruco. Nevertheless, in continuing to strive to be free, at the end of August 1791, an enormous revolt by captive Africans erupted in the plain around Cap Français. By the end of September, over 1,000 plantations had been burned, and their owners killed.[6] Le Cap Français had a large population of freed Africans, and some of them would later become important leaders in the 1791 slave rebellion and Haitian revolution.[7]

In the midst of an era of African revolt and struggle, however, the "memetic ideation" of the French allowed them only to see the great commercial benefit derived from the enslavement of Africans. This ideation coupled with an arrogant belief that their

superiority (meme) guaranteed that the enterprise of slave impor-
tation would be permanent led the Marquis of Larnage, Charles
Burnier, to found the city of "Port-au-Prince" in 1749 and name it
the capital of Saint Domingue. Now no longer the haven of pirates
and rogues, Port-de-Paix became Port-au-Prince, the center of
France's aristocratic (meme) commercial venture grounded in
African enslavement (meme). In less than two years after the
establishment of Port-au-Prince, uncontrollable rebellions sprang
up all over northern Saint Domingue. Jacob Carruthers[8] identified
the source of these rebellions as the "Irritated Genie." The idea of
"genie," however, can only be fully understood through the wisdom
and insight derived from both African and European etymology.

From late Middle English, the origin of the word "genie" is
found in "gignere" meaning "begat." The sense of the word's
meaning was the "spirit attendant on a person" or the spirit which
gives rise to a person's characteristic disposition. French (mid-
17th century) etymology traces the word "genie" to the Latin
"genius," which denoted a "guardian or protective spirit." The Arab
lineage of the word is "Jinn" or "Djinn," who were thought to be supernatural creatures that together with humans and angels made
up the three sentient creatures of Allah. The Djinn were described
as intelligent spirits of lower rank than angels, who were able to
possess human beings and/or appear in human or animal forms.
The Qur'an refers to the Jinn as ethereal beings like the angels
(71:1, 2580).[9] In terms of African cosmological beliefs, there are
parallel beliefs about beings in the spiritual realm. These spiritual
beings guide and protect the lives of the living.

One fails fully to comprehend the real source and success of
the Haitian Revolution when one assumes that the captive African
had no deep philosophical ideas upon which to draw. For the most
part, the arrogance of European hegemony posits that African
men and women were no more than unthinking reactors to external conditions. To the contrary, the idea of an "Irritated Genie" is
most suitable in the context of African spiritual and cosmological
beliefs. The Africans kidnapped, held against their will, and constantly tortured and tormented in Saint Domingue very likely held

beliefs consistent with the idea of spirit guides or protective spirits, i.e., Genie or Djinn. The West African Fon, Ewe, Nago, Igbo, Aja, etc., all carried beliefs in spirit beings that protect and guide the lives of the living. The Yoruba-speaking Nago, for instance, strongly believed in the Rada spirits while those captive Africans from the Kongo understood and respected the Petwo and Kongo spirits. In regards to the notion of "genie" or protective spirit, the Yoruba who found themselves enslaved in Hispaniola must have, in fact, called upon their African spiritual beliefs (e.g., Ori, Ojiji) to understand and mediate their condition. In both the visible and invisible realms, the spirit force of the African was angered, antagonized, provoked, and inflamed.

Dr. Carruthers is correct when he notes that the "Irritated Genie" of Haiti was called forth during the celebration of Ogun's ceremony on August 14, 1791." It should be additionally noted that Ogun (or Ogoun, Ogou) is the Lwa who presides over fire, iron, politics, and war and is the husband of Erzulie. Clearly, Boukman, the Vodou priest, recognized that the African guardian spirits had been angered or irritated. He understood that the launching of a war of liberation was guaranteed success when it coincided with the recognition of the Vodon pantheon, particularly Ogun, and was in congruence with both African cosmological forces and ancestral spiritual beliefs.

Before revisiting the continuous revolts of enslaved Africans that led up to the Haitian revolution, there is a need to first discuss the question of African spiritual systems and demonstrate their collective affinity to and reflection as Vodou.[10] Seven major areas of Africa were invaded and assaulted by European savagery[11]. These areas were, in fact, populated by a self-conscious people whose memetic ideation took into account that special forces or powers governed the world and the lives of people living within it. This core African idea represents the basic notion fundamental to the African sensorial-information structure and emblematic symbolism.

The memetic ideation of the ancient Fon Vodon,[12] later to become Haitian Vodou, was grounded on the BaNtu-Kongo belief

that diverse forces and waves of energy govern life around humans. BaNtu people inhabit most of the continent of Africa and
historically were the founders of highly developed socio-cultural
and political entities ranging from the rainforests of West and Central Africa to the plains and Kalahari Desert of Southern Africa.[13]
The BaNtu-Kongo believe that the heated force of Kalunga blew
up and down as a huge storm of projectiles, *Kimbwandende*,
producing a huge mass in fusion. The fire-force called *Kalunga*
is complete in and of itself and emerges within the emptiness or
nothingness and becomes the source of life on Earth. In the process of cooling the mass in fusion, solidification occurs giving birth
to the Earth.[14]

In effect, the BaNtu believe that all of reality (Kalunga) is fundamentally a process of perpetual and mutual sending and receiving of spirit (energy) in the form of waves and radiations. Kalunga
or reality is the totality, the completeness of all life. It is an ocean
of energy, a force in motion. Kalunga is everything, sharing life
and becoming life continually after life itself. As the totality or the
complete living, Kalunga is comprised of both a visible realm (Ku
Nseke) and an invisible realm (Ku Mpemba). The visible physical
world has spirit (energy) as its most important element. Referred
to as Nkisi (medicine), the spirit element of the physical (visible)
world has the power to care, cure, heal, and guide. The invisible
(spiritual) world (Ku Mpemba) is comprised of human experience, ancestor experience, and the soul-mind experience. The
Ku Mpemba has spirit (energy) as its most important element. In
effect, if reality (visible and invisible) is, it is spirit. BaNtu-Kongo
thought is, therefore, essential to our understanding of African
sensorial-information structures and emblematic symbolism.

By exploring the language and logic of African deep thought as
expressed by the Guinea coast people of the Bight of Benin and
the West Central African Kongo people, one is able to uncover the
African mind, memetic ideation, and its import for understanding
Vodou and the Haitian revolution. Our understanding of the role
or influence of the sensorial-information structures of Vodou can
be assisted by the epistemology of representation and the hidden

psychology of art as emblematic symbolism wherein forms, signs, and symbols reveal hidden meanings, codes, conventions, and conditions, which provoke feelings and behaviors.

Sherry Ortner[15] notes that emblematic symbols have the effect of summing up, expressing a powerful saying, and representing in an emotionally powerful way what the thought system means to a people. Emblematic symbols invoke a complexity of ideas and feelings and an array of metaphoric meanings communicated by the different elements composing the emblem. In effect, the emblematic symbol is an expression that "stands for" and invokes all at once the ideas and feelings reflected in the symbol, including the "logical" relations embedded in the symbol. It is most intriguing that in the realm of Haitian Vodou's African ancestry, almost all the spiritual systems have practices and terminology representing an African sensorial-information structure that was essentially designed to capture the idea that hidden in the image or symbol are powerful forces, which can influence behavior, i.e., to heal or to make ill.

Vodou first appeared in western literature in 1658 in a work written[16] by the ambassador of the Aja-Evhe King of Allada and presented to the court of Phillip IV of Spain. It is noteworthy that this document was written in both Spanish and Ayizo. The cultural-linguistic family of the Ayizo includes the Fon, Aja, and Evhe, etc. In mentioning Vodou over sixty times, the Allada treatise associates Vodou with that which is sacred; i.e., the gods, sacra, priestly, etc.

In discussing Haitian Vodou, many identify the practice of Vodou in Haiti as belonging to separate nations, i.e., Rada, Petwa, Kongo, etc., with separate though sometimes overlapping expressions (Loa).[17] In actuality, Vodoo is essentially an African understanding of spirit (Loa) with various expressions reflecting different experiences. The key to understanding Vodou and the Haitian revolution is to understand it with an African mind.

In Benin (ancient Dahomey), the Fon, Ayizi, Aja, and Evhe utilize the idea of "Bo" (power or energy) to create artistic figures called "Bocio."[18] "Bo" means empowered and "Cio" means body or cadaver. The "Bocio" object is a memetic ideation of an empowered body. It was believed that the "Bo" protected and directed human affairs. The "Bo" represented the idea of the "power to activate" and was conceived symbolically as being gods in the earth —little forest spirits (Aziza), fetishes, and orisas.

The term "Bo" in Aja, Evhe, and Fon conceptualizations is in actuality associated with what it means to be human. "Bo," in this memetic ideation, is linked to "the clearing of the forest." Among the Evhe, the forest clearing (gbo) is thought of as the place where man penetrates in order to plant his seed and returns to gather new life (produce). As such the idea of "clearing of the forest" is not seen as an act but as a place of heightened mystical (sexual) power. This place (gbo) is a crossroad between the human world and the realm of the supernatural. The Evhe believe that the idea of clearing the forest is also linked to the conception of the heavens, which is the abode ("place of rest") of the ancestors. The guardian of this place or field is a female goddess called "Bomena;" "na" means mother, "me" means "in," and "Bo" means "field." Hence, Bomena means "mother in the field." The female goddess Bomena also provides each human with the breath of life, which is also called gbo.

The idea of "Bo" representing cleared fields and the female giver of life goddess suggests that "Bo" connotes a vital source of life as well as the human capacity to cross or pass between the realm of the ancestors and the spirits and the realm of humans. In the African mind or sensorial-information structures, "Bo" constitutes a memetic ideation of the sacredness of life, time, and locale. It delimits and crosses temporal plains while simultaneously framing and interpreting various spatial and spiritual realms.

Psychologically, the "Bo" is a sign that encourages humans to understand and utilize that which is invisible in the visible. The "Bo" represents the potentiality of all human action to uncover the hidden potentiality of all things. In the vocabulary of the Fon, "Boko" means knowledgeable in "Bo." The word "Bokomon" means master of "bo" knowledge. The word for Vodou priestess,

"Mambo," is derived from the Fon word "Nanbo," which means mother (na) of "bo." "Lo" means mystery and "lon" means heaven.

The deep thought of the Guinea coast people of the Bight of Benin and the West Central African Kongo can be seen as African memetic ideation. African memetic ideation results in a symbiotic infection of human consciousness so as to support behaviors that reinforced and propagated beliefs in a deeper meaning in everything. Spirit is essential, a powerful invisible process that influences behavior; living ancestor spirits continue to be involved with the living and are capable of utilizing the invisible (mysteries).

So, in effect, on a deeper intellectual and philosophical level, the master and mother of the Bo, "Bo komon" and "Bo mena," brought together the science of the African Spirit to spark the Haitian revolution via the energy (spirit) vibrations embedded in the "Irritated Genie" (lwa).

Starting with Francois Mackandal, the Haitian revolution has never been analyzed from the mindset and philosophical perspective of the very Africans who engaged in one of the greatest feats of human liberty. Unfortunately, Mackandal remains a historical enigma due to the fact that to accurately document his significance would belie the belief in white supremacy at its root. Hence, the historical and contemporary treatment of his ideas, beliefs, and accomplishments are left vacant because acknowledging them would require the simultaneous release of the falsity of European and American racial dominance.

History informs us that the Haitian Maroon leader, Francois Mackandal,[19] was a very charismatic and influential guerilla leader, who was able to unite different Maroon communities where Africans were held captive on various plantations. Mark Davis[20] suggests that he lived during the 18th century when the Trans-Atlantic Slave Trade was at its peak and that he led an uprising on the French Colony of Saint Domingue (now Haiti and the Dominican Republic). While his particular origin in Africa is not known, some believe him to have come from Senegal, Mali, or Guinea.

Mackandal came from Guinea. Guinea, however, was a euphemism of colonists for all of West Africa, including Senegal and Mali, from where most of the Africans came. Carolyn Fick discusses the possibility that Mackandal came from Makanda, the chief village of the Loango Kingdom in the ancient Kongo since slaves were often named after their villages. It is very likely Mackandal was, in fact, from this region since a large percentage of the captured Africans taken to Saint Domingue in the mid-18th century were from this area. Also, two men, Teysselo and Mayombe, who became his closest confidants, had names the same as regions just to the north of Loango. The Loango Kingdom was established around the 12th century as one of a cluster of equatorial African kingdoms. Loango was in full engagement with Europeans and global trade by the 16th century. As a metropolitan center of its time, we are told that in addition to the King's residence, Loango featured a huge market where artisans, smiths, map makers, potters, bead makers, carpenters, vintners, fishermen, and canoe makers sold their wares. Early ethnographers depicted Loango as including the king's palace, wives' compound, crier's tower, royal wine house, royal dining house, public audience court, royal garden, and wives' garden. Hence, Mackandal may have come from a region of Equatorial Africa that was accustomed to several hundred years of sophisticated cultivation of urbane living.

In this regard, Davis, in quoting Fick, notes that it was highly probable that an important family in the Kongo, who placed a priority on education[21], raised Mackandal and that he told associates that his father had been a tribal chief. He spoke fluent Arabic and could also read and write it. He also knew music, sculpture, and painting. He apparently had a comprehensive knowledge of herbs and plants, which he put to use on the plantation in medicinal applications.

The French aristocrats of Saint Domingue were very troubled that Mackandal had learned to speak French. Since education was strictly forbidden for slaves, they were at a loss to explain his seemingly uncharacteristic brilliance and eloquence. Seeing slaves as animals and focused on labor was critical to the health of the trade. The charismatic oratory for which Mackandal was known would therefore be considered a serious threat. Mackandal was taken from his village (some accounts say as a hostage) at the age of 12 and brought to the Slave Coast to be sold. The ship brought him and many other Africans to Le Cap (Cap Francais then, Cap Haitian now) on the north coast of Saint Domingue, the largest individual market for Africans in the new world and where 24 percent of all Africans were taken.

Other historians (James, Gibbs, Korngold, Heinl, and others) write that Mackandal was brought to Haiti sometime between 1745-1750. He was enslaved on a plantation in Limbe about 20 miles from Le Cap owned by Lenormand de Mezy, one of the largest plantation owners on the island. There he worked doing what most did, harvesting sugar in the crippling heat of the Caribbean to meet the huge and growing worldwide demand.

Fick, citing an article written by M. de C. in *Le Mercure de France* dated September 15, 1789, says a fellow Maroon reported that Mackandal escaped his bonds as he was being tortured. He was sentenced to a punishment of 50 lashes reportedly because he was in love with a beautiful enslaved woman who was coveted by the white master. Fifty lashes with the knotted leather whip were considered a death sentence as each lash flayed the flesh, lifting it off the body. Somehow Mackandal mysteriously escaped before or during this punishment and fled into the hills and the safety of the secret societies of Maroons. Fick believes he began his 12-year career as a revolutionary after he escaped this inhuman torture. Mackandal was considered witty, charming, and confident in his position as a doctor, and he constantly raised the morale of the captive Africans around him. Legend holds that the enslaved and the French far and wide apparently sought his skills.

Mackandal was, also, influential in the Maroon communities, and as a Maroon, he evaded capture for at least ten years. It is believed that he created a network of secret organizations connecting the Maroons with the enslaved. Given his knowledge of the fauna and flora of the island, it is very likely that Mackandal was a Bokor or Houngan or educated by a Bokor once enslaved. As a Bokor who was knowledgeable about the Bo, Mackandal's memetic ideations would have supported the idea of the invisible being greater than the visible and the visible world being comprised of the human experience, ancestor experience, and soul-mind experience in accord with each other. As a Bokor, he would have also understood the invisible power in nature's plants and would have known that that power (bo) could be used to both protect and direct human affairs, including the fight for freedom. Mackandal's plan was to distribute poison to enslaved Africans with instructions to add it to the meals and refreshments they served to the plantation owners and masters. He conducted open schools on poison and folk medicine and used the enslaved on plantations for his secret army.

With the onset of Lenormand de Mezy's and other plantation owners' sickness and death, Mackandal's plan was to raid the plantations at night, torch the property, and kill all the owners. We are told that Mackandal created poisons from island herbs. He chose his army from both slaves and free Blacks, relying heavily on the "pacotilleurs." These were free Blacks that went from plantation to plantation visiting slaves in their quarters to sell them cheap trinkets from Europe.[22] They alone had open access to most plantations throughout the colony. Mackandal encouraged the Maroons to raid plantations at night, torch property, and kill the owners. He believed his singular purpose was to unite all African people in the cause of liberation and the ending of slavery. The French feared that he would drive all whites from the colony. Mackandal's guerilla warfare must have spread great fear and insecurity among the plantation owners. In response to Mackandal's threat, thousands of Blacks were tortured and killed, and the French learned some of the details of Mackandal's revolt, which ultimately led to his capture.

The circumstances surrounding his murder are equally clouded. One accounting of Mackandal's murder claims that he was tied up and bound in the office of the Dufresne Plantation while workers were sent to get the authorities. During this time, he freed himself and escaped. Later, we are told that he was tracked down by dogs, captured and taken to prison in Cap Francais, and given a mock trial. Africans from all over the colony were brought to the town to witness the execution. Mackandal was chained to a stake to be burned alive on January 20, 1758. According to Korgold, after the fire was lit, Mackandal once again freed himself but collapsed in the flames. The oral tradition in Haiti, according to Davis, held that Mackandal died around the age of 30.

Legend has it that Mackandal told his followers that he was immortal, would be reincarnated as a deadly "mosquito," and come back and do more damage than ever before. Some of his contemporaries claimed he disappeared and became the "mosquito" or other flying creature as he had promised. Oral histories of the enslaved suggest that the French recaptured him and threw him back into the fire, but the Africans reported that he fled and was never seen again by anyone. Parenthetically, Davis notes that a massive plague of "mosquitos" carrying yellow fever arrived in swarms during the 1794 revolution to bring death to more than 30,000 British and French troops trying to take Haiti back from the revolutionaries. It was one of the major reasons for the success of the Blacks.

It is of interest that almost all of the historical debate concerning Mackandal centers around the question of his actual leadership and the role African spirituality may have played in his success. This is of interest because the review of Mackandal's place in history may be equally influenced by the European memetic ideas that held Africans to be inferior and thus incapable of serving as the agents of willful and organized liberation. Similarly the prevailing sensoria-information structure of the mind of the master class would find it difficult, if not fearfully incomprehensible, to recognize an inspirational and bonding component of Voudon African spirituality. However, consider that starting with Mackandal, African sensorial information structures, i.e., African memes, supported the idea that the leader is one who is recognized as an adherent or devotee of a powerful spirit driven reality. Hence, Mackandal's legitimacy as a leader would be found in his connection to the power of spirit as evidenced by his knowledge of the secret power (the invisible found in the visible) found in plants to heal or kill. His very stature as a Bokor (one knowledgeable of the

Bo, the sacred) was a memetic sign in the sensoria information structures of the minds in both the Maroon and enslaved African communities. The Bokor was seen as the mouthpiece of the invisible spirits or deities. Hence the words and instruction coming from a Bokor were literal symbols that "symbiotically infected" the African mind and dictated behavior consistent with the memetic idea. As a Voudonist, Mackandal served as a living symbol and sign of the idea of being free and African. The behavior consistent with Mackandal's memetic ideation would be behavior characterized by resistance, revenge, and revolt. His public torture and murder can also be seen as an attempt to plant in the minds of the Africans an alternate sensoria-information structure of all powerful, unforgiving, brutal, and savage planters and master class requiring total submission. The savage murder of Francois Mackandal did not, however, kill the memetic ideation of the Vodou spirit or quest to live as free spirits in alignment with a divinely governed natural world.

The "Mackandal Revolution" of 1750 was unique in all of history, and it proceeded and nurtured the final "Haitian Revolution" that began with Toussaint L'Ouverture in 1791 and ended with Jacques Dessalines in 1804. The Revolution of 1791 remains the only successful revolution by African slaves in history. However, in the story of African freedom, what is obscured or misunderstood is that the Haitian revolution of 1791 and 1804, along with Mackandal's quest for freedom, should be seen as one continuous African struggle for the right to be free and African. It was a continuous struggle seeded by Mackandal, irritated by Boukman, reignited by Toussaint, and further carried forth by Dessalines.

Given the undying struggle to be free and African, sometime during the thirty years after Mackandal's murder, Dutty Boukman, a Jamaican-born Houngan[23] who had been enslaved by the British, was sold to the French in Saint Domingue. Impressed by his intelligence and commanding stature, the French made Boukman a "commandeur," a so-called slave driver and later a coach driver. Blinded by arrogance, the French were unable to recognize Boukman's identity as a master of the knowledge of Bo or to see that the African spirit of a Bokomon would turn the role of commandeur into that of a liberator. Along with Cecile Fatiman, a mulatto Voudon mambo (nanbo, mother of Bo), Boukman inspired the people and on August 14, 1791, conducted a freedom ceremony at the Bois Caimen. The prophecy, which occurred during the ceremony, was that three enslaved Africans, Jean François Papillon, George Bissou, and Jeanot Bullet, would free all the Africans in Saint Domingue. The ceremony ended with Boukman and Fatiman leading the gathering in a blood oath to take revenge against their French oppressors and cast aside the image of the oppressor's God. According to the Encyclopedia of African Religion, "blood from the animal, and some say from humans as well, was given in a drink to the attendees to seal their fates in loyalty to the cause of liberation of Saint Domingue."[24] A week later 1,800 plantations had been destroyed, and 1,000 plantation owners killed.

Like the history of Mackandal, the significance of Bois Caimen is shrouded with debate. Its significance to the onset of the Haitian revolution may, however, be better revealed by treating it as an event pregnant with sensorial-information structures, which symbiotically infected the African mind and encouraged behavior that reinforced ideas proposed by the sensorial-information structure.

Historical commentary on the Bois Caimen Ceremony is rich with debate concerning its role and relevance to the onset of the Haitian revolution. A good deal of discussion centers on its location, timing, actions, and significance for the revolution. Since very little analyses of the event have been conducted from the perspective of the Africans, contributing to the alleged controversies, doubts, and challenges reflected in the different interpretations of the historical record serves little purpose. However, it should be noted that most accounts of the Bois Caimen Ceremony suggest that:

> During the night of 14 August 1791 in the midst of a forest called Bois Caimen [Alligator Wood], on the Morne Rouge in the northern plain, the slaves held a large meeting to draw up a final plan for a general revolt. They consisted of about two hundred slave drivers, sent from various plantations in

the region. Presiding over the assembly was a Black man named Boukman, whose firy words exalted the conspirators. Before they separated, they held amidst a violent rainstorm an impressive ceremony, so as to solemnize the undertakings they made. While the storm raged and the lightning shot across the sky, a tall Black woman appeared suddenly in the center of the gathering. Armed with a long, pointed knife that she waved above her head, she performed a sinister dance singing an African song, which the others faced down against the ground, repeated in chorus. A black pig was then dragged in front of her and she split it opened with her knife. The animal's blood was collected in a wooden bowl and served still foaming to each delegate. At a signal from the priestess, they all threw themselves on their knees and swore blindly to obey the orders of Boukman, who had been proclaimed the supreme chief of the rebellion. He announced as his choice of principal lieutenants Jean-Francois Papillon, George Biassou and Jeanot Bullet.[25]

What we are told is that Cecile Fatiman, a Voudon Mambo helped with the ceremony along with another Mambo named Marinette, who actually sacrificed the black pig at the ceremony. In closing this ceremony, Dutty Boukman is reported to have given the following prayer:

The God who created the sun which gives us light, who rouses the waves and rules the storm, though hidden in the clouds, he watches us. He sees all that the white man does. The God of the white man inspires him with crime, but our God calls upon us to do good works. Our God who is good to us orders us to revenge our wrongs. He will direct our arms and aid us. Throw away the symbol of the god of the whites who has so often caused us to weep, and listen to the voice of liberty, which speaks in the hearts of us all.[26]

Clearly, two significant events did occur. The first occurred around August 14th and was composed of members of the enslaved elite (coachmen, house servants, commandeurs, etc.) from over 100 different plantations. Parenthetically, the term "slave elite" requires special commentary. Applying the idea or classification of an "elite class" of people who are enslaved is an anachronism. The hierarchy of class and the values consistent with it are congruent with the memetic ideations of European culture. To classify the coachmen, house servants, commandeurs, and field servants as elite and the other enslaved as a "lower" or a more common form of enslavement is an imposition of western thought onto the African mind. From the enslaved Africans' consciousness, they were captives without freedom and constantly being dehumanized, demeaned, and tormented regardless of tasks, gender, or age. The corrosive imposition of European memetic meanings of human relationships, roles, responsibilities, and rights is an ongoing unexamined legacy of the clash of European and African consciousness.

The first meeting took place in Plaine du Nord parish on the Leonard de Mezy plantation and estate, which was located at the foot of the Red Mountains. At this meeting, at which Toussaint L'Ouverture was very likely in attendance, the so-called slave elite made the decision to rebel against their oppressors. Another meeting occurred about ten kilometers to the east of the Leonard de Mezy Plantation at a place called Caimen, most likely on the Marquis de Choisseul Plantation. The Lagon á Cayman was a swamp surrounded by woods spanning the Choiseul and Duston Plantations where the Bois Caimen Ceremony most likely took place. Some believe that before carrying out their plan of insurrection, the so-called slave elite celebrated with a festival and sacrifice in the midst of a wooded and non-cultivated area on the Choisseul Plantation called Le Caimen (French for "the alligator").

The Bois Caimen Ceremony involved Africans from the Northern Province who were a mixture of West Central African BaNtu-Kongo and Guinea Coast (Aja, Fon, Evhe, etc). Some suggest that the pig was surrounded with "fetishes" and sacrificed to "the all-powerful spirit of the black race," and after it was sacrificed, participants took hairs from the pig as "protective amulets." What seems to be missed by most commentary is that the decision of these men and women (believed to be Creole dominated) to launch a war of liberation had to be spiritually sanctioned and ratified by the larger African family and the ancestors. Hence, the Bois Caimen Ceremony could be viewed as the spiritual verification and solidification of the decisions to go to war. Hence, the significance of Vodou and African spirituality should be revisited in the interpretation of Bois Caimen and the onset of the Haitian revolution.

When reviewed as a dramatic expression of a sensorial-information structure, this critical moment in Haiti's history can be further illuminated. The philosophical and spiritual beliefs of the BaNtu Kongo peoples (Fon, Ayizo, Aja, Evhe) from the Bight of Benin along the Guinea Coast of West Africa is the lens through which this event should be viewed.

Revisiting the Alligator Swamp

As a Vodou ceremony, Bois Caimen would have been regulated by the spirits belonging to families of "nanchons" (nations) identified as Rada, Petro, Nago, Kongo, and Ghede. The Rada spirits (loa), whose color is white, are older and associated with the gods of Africa. The Rada loa include Legba, Luko, Ayizan, Anaisa, Pye, Damballah Vedo, Ayida-Weddo, Erzulie Fredu, La Sirene, and Agwe. The Petro loa, whose color is red, include Erzulie Dantor, Marinette, and Ogoun Kalfu. The Kongo loa are believed to originate from the Kongo region of Africa and include the Simbi loa and the fierce and feared female loa Marinette. The Nago loa are thought to be from Nigeria and include the Ogoun spirits. Finally, the Ghede loa are the spirits of the dead; i.e., those who have lived already and have nothing to fear.

For the most part, the recorders of Haitian history profoundly disrespected African ways. As such, they claimed that Cecile Fatiman performed a "sinister dance" singing an African song with the other Africans, faced down against the ground, repeated in chorus wherein, a black pig was then "dragged" in front of her to be sacrificed. This African Mambo priestess ignited the collective spirit of all those gathered on that fateful night. At a signal from the priestess, all the Africans threw themselves on their knees and swore "blindly" to obey the orders of Boukman. The ceremony was, however, neither sinister nor were the participants blindly obeying Boukman. Rather than being blindly obedient, they were active participants in their own fight for liberation.

Cecile Fatima was the daughter of an African woman and a Corsican prince. She and her mother were sold, perhaps by her Corsican father, into slavery in Saint Domingue. As a Vodou priest, she became a mother of the "Bo," Mambo. The respect and power given to her by the Africans is evidenced by her authority in naming Boukman, Jean-Francois, Bissou, and Jeanot as the initial leaders of the revolt. She became the wife of Jean-Louis Michel Pierrot, who led the Black battalion in the last great battle of the war (i.e., the battle of Vertiers). Given her power, it is very probable that she was there alongside her husband.

From an African episteme, the Bois Caimen ceremony would have been opened by calling upon Papa Legba, who is considered the voice of God; and his presence at the ceremony would have supported the memetic ideation that "the gate between the world of the living and the mysteries was opened." Old men on crutches and walking with canes wearing straw hats smoking pipes and strutting with dogs would have signaled the presence and memetic ideation of Papa Legba. He is considered the intermediary between the spirits (loa) and humanity. He alone stands at the spiritual crossroads and gives (or denies) permission to speak with the spirits of Guinea. As the gatekeeper between the world of the living and the mysterious, Papa Legba opens and closes the doorway between humans and spirits and usually appears as an old man on a crutch and leaves wearing a straw hat and smoking a pipe or sprinkling water. The dog is sacred to him.

In addition, Damballah would have had to be present at the Bois Caimen Ceremony because Damballah, a Radu spirit, is the most important of all the loa. He is a root (Rada) spirit and is depicted as a serpent or snake. He, along with his wife/companion Ayido Vedo (the rainbow serpent), is considered to be the loa of creation. In Rada form, Damballah makes the sound of a hissing snake. In Petro form, he speaks through a flame or fire and is called "Damballah nan Flambo." In addition to drumming, the ceremony would have been replete with sounds of hissing snakes and flickering fire flames. Damballah Nan Flambo would have been present. The deeper meaning associated with Damballah is found in the ideas of serpent, root, rainbow, creation, hissing, and flame/fire. Hissing represents a noise made by an angry or frustrated animal, ergo, a serpent. The serpent, as a signifier of Damballah, is a profound and deep orienting idea. Serpents are represented as potent guardians of temples and other sacred spaces. When threatened, snakes hold and defend their ground. Thus, they are natural guardians of treasures or sacred sites, which cannot easily be moved out of harm's way. The serpent is considered one of the wisest animals. Serpents have the qualities of vengefulness and vindictiveness. The serpent also represents the container or instrument of its venom that has the power to heal, poison, or provide expanded consciousness. The crackling sound of fire is also important. Technically "fire" is the rapid oxidation of a material in the chemical process of combustion releasing heat, light, and various products. The positive effects of fire include stimulating growth and maintaining various ecological systems. As a memetic ideation, fire represents the ability to change and release a new condition or status.

Given the overwhelming use of Africans from the Kongo as field workers, the Simbi loa would probably have dominated the ceremony. The Simbi are associated with water and memetic ideation and speak to communication and magical powers found in leaves (i.e. poison). The Simbi loa require special mention. In Kongo spirituality there is a recognized spiritual hierarchy. Immediately above living humans are the ancestors or Nkuyu. These are the ancestors who are named. Above them, and more removed from humans, are the Simbi. In the Kongo belief system, all Simbi (also called Basimbi for plural and Kisimbi) are associated with water. They are the source of special blessings but are known to be somewhat unpredictable. They are also said to be "twice born," which means that they have not lived recently on earth. They represent a higher class of ancestors, having been elevated by death to a higher status than humans, yet still available to us for consultation and service. Simbi is also a Loa of communication. Phenomena involving communication, which moves at the speed of light, are in Simbi's domain (e.g., nerve impulses, Internet, electricity.) Unlike the great serpent Damballah Wedo, Simbi is considered to be a long, slim snake. Simbi is a very special Loa in the Vodou pantheon. He shares characteristics with all the major deities and all the primary principles of the entire spiritual system. Essentially a Kongo spirit, Simbi represents both the Rada and Petwa incarnations. Simbi is a crossroad Loa symbolized as a snake in a field of equally armed crosses. Simbi is, above all, the preeminent magicians and is considered the patron of all the magic. He radiates in every direction and is the statesman and wise soul who brings power, wealth, and insight to his servitors. The original simbis were cool, creative spirits in the Kongo cosmology. These include Simbi Dlo (Simbi in Water) and Simbi Andezo (Simbi in Two Waters). The magical ability of their power, called "nkisi" in Kongolese, translated into powerful medicine or magic that was then used in Petro rites, giving rise to Simbi Anpaka, Simbi Ganga, and Simbi Makaya to name but a few. Every Simbi also has specific associations. Simbi Andezo has a connection to both fresh and salt water. Simbi Anpaka is associated with leaves and poisons. Simbi is sometimes portrayed as having one foot or no feet at all, yet is extremely agile in climbing trees[27].

The one Loa all historians agree to have been present was Cecile Fatiman's Loa, Erzulie Dantor. Erzulie Dantor is a warrior spirit whose memetic ideation is to be a fierce protector of women and children. The presence of buxom women holding children in their arms with, most likely, weapons (knives) held up high was very likely the common signage or indicator of the ceremony.

As noted in Chapter 3, sensorial-information structures (memes) are contagious information patterns in the form of symbols, ideas, sounds, and movements that are capable of being perceived by any of the senses and replicated by symbiotically entering the mind and thus alter behaviors in ways that propagate the idea, symbol, etc. Both Boukman and Fatima are key "signs" in the Bois Caimen Ceremony. As key elements of a Vodou ceremony, the Loas, Legba, Damballah, La Sirene, Agwe, Erzulie Dantor, Marinette, and Ogoun, Simbi, etc., are also key signs and ideas, capable of propagating certain beliefs and behaviors. Accordingly, in terms of human consciousness and memetic ideation, the Bois Caimen Ceremony can be viewed as the interplay of an African cultural inheritance in response to European (Spanish and French) domination.

Correspondingly, as an African narrative drama, the Bois Caimen vodou ceremony, can be seen as a set of contagious information patterns, which symbiotically inoculated the African mind so as to support behaviors antithetical to enslavement. As such, the event could be seen as a climatic spark between African and European culture and consciousness. In effect, the African memetic ideation compelled behaviors that challenged the continued support of conduct that European memetic ideation demanded (e.g. dehumanization, subordination, and inferiority, etc.) It would be short-sighted to not recognize that the African cultural inheritance of the enslaved Africans also included contagious information patterns in the form of symbols, sounds, and movements, which served as orienting ideas that shaped as well as instigated behaviors.

Thusly, the Bois Caimen Ceremony would have been where the elite enslaved Africans received spiritual ratification for their planned revolt. It would have been where a mixture of about 200 hundred enslaved Africans from West Central African (BaNtu-Kongo) and Guinea Coast (Aja, Fon, and Evhe, etc.) held a large meeting to draw up a final plan for a general revolt. The Voudon Mambo Cecile Fatiman and Dutty Boukman, a master of the Bo, led the Bois Caimen Ceremony. Papa Legba, who stands at the spiritual crossroads and gives permission to speak to the spirits of Guinea, had to have been invoked. Damballah, the most important of all the Loa, would have had to be present also along with his wife/companion Ayido Vedo, (the rainbow serpent). The Simbi Loa would probably have dominated the ceremony.

In revisiting Bois Caimen, as noted earlier, the start of the Haitian revolution ended with the sacrifice of a black pig, a blood oath of loyalty, and a prayer of destiny. In further dissecting the drama of Bois Caimen and the loa present, one finds, for instance, the following orienting symbols, ideas, sounds, and movements as memetic ideations: woman, breast, child, black pig, screeching owl, rainbow serpent, hissing, flame/fire, dogs, old men, magic, ancestors, crossroads, communication, knives, blood, waves, twice born, armed crosses, stems, light, revenge, liberty, and hearts. To fully appreciate the significance of Bois Caimen, one has to further explore the deeper meaning of the features, attributes, and characteristics of these orienting ideas embedded in the drama and then reconstruct the meaning of the event from its memetic ideation.

In the Bois Caimen drama, *"while the storm raged and the lightning shot across the sky, a tall Black woman, Cecile Fatiman, whose Loa, Erzulie Dantor, depicted as a scarred and boxumly woman holding a child in one hand and a knife in the other, appeared."* The deeper meaning of "woman" as memetic ideation is especially significant. As a sign, woman means one who is capable of bearing offspring with the following qualities or aspects: gentleness, sensitivity, compassion, sympathy, tenderness, insight, warmth, yielding, softness, nurturance, grace, communication, intuition, emotion, close, warm, mother, homemaker, quiet, and passive. Characteristically, woman as memetic ideation is inwardly oriented, responsive, cooperative, conservative, and relational. As an orienting idea, woman has the ability to bring various elements and components together to create energy. It is the power of the feminine to use intuition, nurture information, and lend emotion, which in turn gives the event and/or its participants the authority to act with wisdom and to have the orientation that what is being done is right and proper.

The color black in the black pig signifies a color that does not emit or reflect light in any part of the visible spectrum. Black represents the absorption of all other frequencies of light. Black has the characteristics of authority and seriousness. The color black in Africa is a symbol of life and prosperity. The pig is an animal possessing a keen and excellent sense of smell. They are omnivores (consume both plants and animals) with large heads and long snouts used to dig into the soil to find food. Pigs/boars are known to defend themselves and their young with intense vigor. The fighting style of the male pig/boar is to lower its head, charge, and slash ferociously upward with his tusks. The female pig/boar charges with her head up, her mouth wide open, and then ferociously bites. The attack of the pig always results in severe trauma, dismemberment, or blood loss. The presence of Damballah at the Bois Caimen Ceremony characterizes the event as sacred time filled with the power to radically change, defend one's essence, seek revenge for the harm done, and release the African. Erzulie Dantor represents a warrior spirit whose deeper meaning is a fierce protector of women and children, ergo the future.

Finally, the deeper meaning of Simbi is found in the ideas of water, twice born, ancestors, communication, leaves, and (lightning) speed. The Simbi represent a higher class of ancestors, having been elevated by death to a higher status and service. Simbi is also associated with the magical power found in leaves as medicine or poison. The deeper meaning of leaves is found in their capacity to store food and water and serve as the site where transpiration (evaporation) and guttation (self-generated water/sap with nutrients) occur. Having the power to evaporate or disappear as well as generate one's own nutrition are qualities of Simbi. The idea of "twice born" has the meaning of bringing forth (as if by birth) in double quantity or degree. It also has the meaning of having undergone a definite experience of fundamental moral and spiritual renewal.

Hence, with the Simbi, the Bois Caimen Ceremony was experienced as having the capacity to bring forth or self-generate a new higher status (e.g. freedom and spiritual renewal). The enslaved Africans from West Central Africa and Guinea Coast would have been well aware that the Bokor (one knowledgeable of the Bo, the sacred), Dutty Boukman, and the Vodou priestess, "Mambo" (mother of "bo", the sacred) Cecile Fatiman were guiding them in sacred space and time to change their status as the wretched of the earth.

In the context of memetic ideation, a reinterpretation of Bois Caimen suggests rather clearly that in this clash of cultures and consciousness, the fundamental propagating idea for the enslaved was to be free and African. However, the European memetic ideation equally infected African consciousness and is the source of the complexity found in the experiences of Haitian independence and contemporary Haitian society.

---

1 See *Haiti-Haiti? Philosophical Reflections for Mental Decolonization* (2011) by Jean-Bertrand Aristide for insightful reflections regarding Haiti's mental decolonization from the perspective of one of Haiti's national leaders.

[2] See Daniel Rasmussen's *American Uprising: The Untold Story of America's Largest Slave Revolt* (2011) for a detailed account of the New Orleans Revolt led by Charles Deslondes and two other enslaved Africans named Quamena and Harvey can be found in. In this text Rasmussen asserts that the Deslondes Revolt was inspired by the Haitian revolution of 1804.

[3] See *Avengers of the New World: The Story of the Haitian Revolution* (2004) by Laurent Dubois for a comprehensive discussion of enslaved Africans striving to be free before the Haitian revolution and also *Flight to Freedom: African Runaways and Maroons in America* (2006) by Alvin O. Thompson.

[4] See The Negro ((2008) by W.E.B. Dubois, who identifies Polydor as a Maroon chief who was succeeded by Francois Mackandal; Also, in *Les Marrons de la Liberté* (1972), Alvin Thompson notes that the details regarding colonial administrators comes solely from the colonists' own reports in their correspondence or from the writings of their own colonial historians. It was through these sources that from the first rebellion in Bahoruco up to the general uprising of the slaves, we have any record of rebellion leaders (e.g., Padrejean) whose intention was to cut the throats of all the Whites in the Northwest and Mackandal who was organizing a mass poisoning and had agents in all points of the colony and projected the elimination of all the whites.

[5] See *Haitian Revolutionary Studies* (2002) by David Patrick Geggus, who highlights one aspect of the role of the French revolution as impetus for the Haitian revolution in pointing out that by refuting the ideology of white supremacy and destroying the governmental structure that imposed it, the French revolution brought the free coloreds to power in Saint Domingue and that this transfer of

power to the free coloreds gained further impetus from the outbreak of the war with England and Spain.

[6]   See *The Haitian Revolution* (1990) by Franklin Knight, who allows us to see during this same period, in the USA, the efforts of Richard Allen and Absalom Jones, along with other Black community leaders, to form their own religious society and the Free African Society in 1787 as parallel developments of Black nationalism.

[7]   From Carruthers, J. (1985, p. 6-18). *The Irritated Genie: An Essay on the Haitian Revolution.*

[8]   See Qur'an, Surah 72 (Sūrat al-Jinn) for a fuller discussion of the meaning of Jinn in Islam.

[9]   The terms Vodon, Vodoun, Voudou, Vodou, and Vodou are often used interchangeably as representing African traditional spiritual systems. Vodon is typically used to denote the spiritual practices of the Fon, Aja, and Evhe people of West Africa. The preferred spelling introduced to the European world was "Vodou" by the King of the Aja-Evhe. Vodou seems to be the spelling most associated with the retention of the Vodou as practiced in Louisiana. Accordingly, to minimize the confusion due to time and place as well as different European (Spanish, French, and English) translations, when referring to the West African spiritual system, the spelling Vodun will be used, and when referring to the spiritual system brought into Saint Domingue, later to be called Haiti, the spelling as Vodou will be used.

[10]   The seven major areas were the Senegambia, Sierra Leone, Gold Coast, Bight of Benin, Bight of Biafra, West Central Africa, and Mozambique. See Gomez, M. (1998). *Exchanging Our Country Marks: The Transformation of African Identities in the Colonial and Anti-Bellum South.*

[11]   Vodou is also spelled vodoun, vodoo, voodoo, vodou, vodoun, vaudoo, and vaudou. It represents a powerful spiritual science (religion) as a way of life driven by a quest for cosmic harmony and oneness with God.

[12]   As a result of the BaNtu expansion, from the Nubian Desert to the Cape of Good Hope and from Senegal to Zanzibar, there is a "philosophical and cultural affinity" among and between the indigenous people of Africa. What should be clear is that this BaNtu expansion represents the migratory movement of both people and their cultural and linguistic inventions. The geographical distribution and temporal order of the BaNtu expansion (language, culture, and spiritual beliefs) also match the geographical distribution of the spread of farming and agriculture, which are key to the establishment of civil society and high culture. Another migration, though unrecognized as an important phase of BaNtu expansion, is the Trans-Atlantic and Trans-Saharan Trade in enslaved peoples.

[13]   See Fu-Kiau, K. (2001). *The Spiritual Knot: African Cosmology of the BaNtu-Kongo*, (2nd Ed.).

[14] See Ortner, S. (1973). "On Key Symbols," *American Anthropologists*, 75(5) pp. 1335-46.

[15] See Blier, S.P. (1995). *African Voodun: Art, Psychology and Power* for a discussion of the correspondence written by the ambassador of the Aja-Evhe, King of Allada.

[16] See Filan, K. (2007, p. 13). *The Haitian Vodou Handbook* for definition and misconception of the idea of Vodou.

[17] See Deren, M. (2007, pp. 16, 88-89). *Divine Horseman: The Living Gods of Haiti* for further discussion of the origin of Voodoun and the nature and power of the Lwa.

[18] One of the best accounts in English is *The Making of Haiti: The Saint Domingue Revolution from Below* (1990, pp. 251-259) by Carolyn Fick. Fick provides the translated testimony of one of the slaves who confessed to being involved in Mackandal's plot. See also Weaver, K. (2006, pp. 77-97). *Medical Revolutionaries: The Enslaved Healers of Eighteenth-Century Saint Domingue*, and Bryan, P. (1984). *The Haitian Revolution and Its Effects*.

[19] Davis, M. (1997). *Francois Mackandal: The True Story, Facts, Myths and Legends*.

[20] Fick, C. (1990, pp. 65-69).

[21] See Asante, M. & Mazama, A. (2008, p.131). *Encyclopedia of African Religion*.

[22] See Asante, M. & Mazama, A. (2008, p. 131).

[23] See Bellegarde, D. (2002, p. 80). "Histoire du People (1492 – 1952)." In D. Geggus. *Haitian Revolutionary Studied*.

[24] Fick, C. (1990, p. 60).

[25] Fick, C. (1990, p. 60).

[26] Fick, C. (1990, p. 60).

[27] See Filan, K. (2007, pp. 154-158). "Chapter 19: Simbi." In *The Haitian Vodou Handbook; Protocols for Riding with the Lwa*.

Chapter Five

The Cache of Consciousness and the Haitian Revolution

The question of consciousness is critical to understanding the psychological underpinnings of the Haitian revolution and the spirit and mindset of the Haitian people today. However, the illumination of the cache of Haitian consciousness must be explored as an extension of the notion and understanding of the consciousness of African people in general. In attempting to understand African consciousness,[1] our immediate task can only be accomplished if we are able to free our thinking from the meanings and constraints imposed by our training in Western memetic ideations. The African heritage of Black people is replete with elegant, elaborate, and extraordinary conceptualizations of human knowing and awareness, ergo consciousness. Before outlining the Cache of Consciousness and the Haitian revolution, a discussion of African consciousness will be offered. The following explication is a brief and partial composite of African-centered understanding of consciousness.

With regard to the notion of consciousness, it is fairly well documented that Africa conceives of reality and all that is within reality as a mental expression of the Divine. In ancient Nile Valley metaphysics, for example, Djehuti (whom the Greeks call Hermes) was considered the mind and will (consciousness) of the creative Demiurge and, from this "personified" Divine mind, emerged the "word" that brings all things into being. What the ancient Africans of the Nile Valley (Kemites) called the "Intelligence of the Heart" was, in fact, an intricate dialogue between the electromagnetic fields generated by the "knowing" cells in our hearts, minds, and bodies, and the electromagnetic energy fields in the world at large, and selected energy fields found in our particular experiences with time, place, and space.

Similarly, Dogon metaphysics states that the universe is the "thought" in the "mind" (consciousness) of Amma, the creator. Directly, in terms of consciousness, the philosophical thinking of the Akan makes a distinction between *"Adwen"* (realms of knowing) as thought, *"Nea Wonhu"* (that which cannot be perceived), and *"Nea edtra Adwen"* (that which transcends thought). The Akan also have a concept called *"Anidho"* (levels of awareness), which represents being conscious with specific dimensions of *"Anidahoso"* (aware-ness of self) and *"Oben"* (perception beyond the ordinary). The Kikongo word for conscious in Lingala is *ezaleli*, which means "the way you are in life," your "essence." The BaNtu-Kongo believe that diverse forces and waves of energy govern life surrounding humans. This fire-force, called *Kalunga*, is complete in and of itself and emerges within the emptiness or nothingness to become the source of life on earth.[2] Thus *Kalunga* as force in motion is con-sidered consciousness. The BaNtu-Kongo believe that the heated force of Kalunga blew up and down as a huge storm of projectiles, *Kimbwandende*, producing a huge mass in fusion. In the process of cooling, solidification occurred giving birth to the earth.[3] In a very real way, the world, as a physical reality floating in *Kalunga*, emerged as an act of consciousness.

Consciousness and identity are inextricably connected. In-cluded in the African notion of identity is the belief that the com-plexity of being "a person" (immaterial and material) gives one an intrinsic human value and that the "person" is, in fact, a "process" characterized by the divinely governed laws of essence, appear-ance, perfection, and compassion. At the human level, identity is always a collective experience and passes from one collective generation (being) to the next. It is the "reincarnation of identity" as psyche that constitutes the reincarnation of a person. A reincar-nated person is a new person only in the carnal sense. The collec-tive identity or what some call racial consciousness is constantly renewed in each succeeding generation.

The African is distinguished by a particular consciousness that is reflected in a special capacity for having intelligence of the mind and heart. Every knowable and perceivable object in the natural universe is a hieroglyph of Divine consciousness (i.e., comprehen-sion and imagination). For the African, consciousness is more than thinking, feeling, and awareness. Everything vibrates in a divinely governed universe. Consciousness is "potentiality" contained within itself. As potentiality contained within itself, the entire know-ing and knowable universe, as a never-ending totality of possibili-ties, is consciousness. Consciousness is, in effect, the intelligent energy of the Divine. With this African notion of consciousness, one should also recognize that the spectrum of consciousness includes numerous levels, which differ only in degree of frequency and density. In fact, the level of consciousness determines the configuration of matter. Level is indicated by vibration. Consciousness, therefore, is inscribed in and determines the nature of every organism. Consciousness is, however, more than potentiality contained within itself. Hence, as a knowing and knowable vibration, motion, or energy, consciousness is simultaneously "potentiality" and "intentionality" contained in the pulse of life.

One should immediately ask, "What was the potentiality and intentionality contained in the consciousness of those men and women who were the cause and consequence of the Haitian revolution?" In this regard, one should recognize that at the human level, consciousness is always a collective experience and passes from one collective generation (being) to the next. Like the energy or vibration indicative of it, consciousness is never destroyed. Being a particular vibratory phenomenon, African people reincarnate consciousness from one generation to the next irrespective of geographical location. This would suggest that the consciousness of the Yoruba, Dahomians, Igbo, Nago, Hausa, Aja, Ewe, Fon BaKongo, and Mandingo etc., was renewed and reshaped as the consciousness of Africans expressing themselves as Haitians. Chester Higgins points out, "We are Africans not because we are born in Africa, but because Africa is born in us."[4] Accordingly, it is important to note in this discussion that, while different groups of people were kidnapped and taken to the Americas, it is the African born in them and not the place in Africa that shaped their African consciousness. The Africa born in Hispaniola is that in-born sense of consciousness, that vibratory fire force in motion that is complete in and of itself yet continually emerging to become the source and the consequence of living.

Unfortunately, it was this African sense of consciousness that was derailed or deformed as the direct and indirect intent and consequence of Arab conquest, American-led international enslavement, and European colonization. The de-Africanization (dehumanization) of the African, which all three foreign powers hold in common, requires the distortion of African consciousness.

The Root of the Haitian Cache of Consciousness

Historiography too often is reduced to a chronology of events with little understanding of the psychology of the men and women who were both the cause and consequence of the events of their times. Historians tell us that the Haitian Revolution (1791-1804) was a period of brutal conflict in the French colony of Saint Domingue leading to the elimination of slavery and the establishment of Haiti as the first republic ruled by people of African ancestry. The Haitian Revolution started in the heavily African-majority northern plains of Saint Domingue in 1791. In 1792, the French government sent three commissioners with troops to reestablish control. They began to build an alliance with the free people of color who wanted more civil rights. In 1793, France and Great Britain went to war, and British troops invaded Saint Domingue. The execution of Louis XVI heightened tensions in the colony. In order to build an alliance with the gens de couleur and those enslaved, the French commissioners Sonthonax and Polverel abolished slavery in the colony.

> *The French name still darkens our plains; everything recalls the remembrance of the cruelties of that barbarous people. Our laws, our customs, our cities, everything bears the characteristics of the French—Hearken to what I say! The French still have footing in our island! ... And what a dishonorable absurdity – conquering in order to be slave.*
>
> *J. Dessalines, January 1, 1804*[5]

Given Dessalines' admonition of 1804 concerning the French influence in a free Haiti as a reflection of consciousness, this chapter will attempt to examine the Haitian Revolution from the mind and consciousness of its major architects. The Cache of Consciousness of the architects of the revolution is far more complex than the chronicling of events. The understanding of African consciousness is critical to a fuller understanding of the Haitian Revolution. There are some critical actors and high points or moments in the story of the Haitian Revolution. However, the Haitian Revolution and its legacy for the Haitian people is better understood when one examines the consciousness of these historical actors and architects of the revolution.

Toussaint L'Ouverture

Francois Dominique Toussaint L'Ouverture was born on November 1, 1743, into slavery on a plantation under the ownership of Count de Breda and was named Toussaint Breda after his master but later changed his name to Toussaint L'Ouverture, which in French, means "all saints" or "all souls opening." Toussaint's father, an Arrada named Gaou-Guinou, was born a free man in Africa but was kidnapped from his native country of Dahomey and brought to the island of Haiti as an enslaved laborer on the lucrative sugar plantations of the Count de Breda. Toussaint was the oldest of eight children—five of which were boys and three of which were girls. The plantation overseer allowed Toussaint the rare privilege of learning to read and write. He was raised as a Roman Catholic and read, amongst other writings, Plutarch, Epictetus, Caesar, Saxe, and Abbé Raynal. While Catholic, Toussaint did not abandon his father's African cultural beliefs. David Geggus points out that Toussaint was probably fluent in the language of his Arrada father, i.e., Ewe-Fon and that he enjoyed using it to speak with members of his own ethnic group, which was very likely Arrada.[6] We are also told that Toussaint, along with Dessalines, served the Voodoo Lwa, Papa Ogu-fe. The Ogou or Ogoun is a Nago Lwa of power. Ogou is the master of the machete and is often seen waving a sabre or machete and visualized as a military general. The colors of the Ogou are blue and red. Parenthetically, Toussaint's general uniform may have more to do with his Voodoo Lwa than the aristocratic image or status of a French military officer.

Toussaint served as a coachman and house servant until he was about 33 and gained his freedom. As a freeman, Toussaint married Suzanne Simone Baptiste[7] in 1782, and together they had three children. The eldest child Placide was probably adopted by Toussaint and is generally thought to be Suzanne's first child with a mulatto. The two sons born of his marriage to Suzanne were

Isaac and Saint Jean. Suzanne and her children were arrested along with Toussaint and placed under the supervision of General Ducos and taken to Port of Brest, France, where they were separated from Toussaint. Suzanne Toussaint was tortured, and most likely molested, starved,[8] and degraded during her captivity.

The memetic ideation found in Toussaint's constitution is informative. In terms of memetic ideation, the Haitian constitution, and for that matter all political constitutions, really serves as a document of cultural discourse designed to reflect and/or influence human consciousness and therein propagate and legitimate the behavioral dispositions of its adherents. The consciousness of Toussaint is, in part, revealed in the Haitian Constitution of 1801,[9] which he authorized and very likely drafted some of its language. The Haitian Constitution of 1801 is, in part, an illumination of the consciousness of Toussaint L'Ouverture. Upon a brief review, one can see that Toussaint's constitution, in some instances, challenged and reflected a complex relationship with the memetic ideation found in the Ancient Regime and the church as an essential component of the three estates. For Toussaint the French mores as cultural discourse shaped and supported the birthing of a new Haitian aesthetic, moral code, and set of human relations. Toussaint's constitution encoded the idea, for instance, of Saint Domingue being part of the French Empire. That Haiti was a French colony and not a free independent state is preserved in this document. The constitution explicitly states, "All men are born, live and die free and French." While the constitution forbade slavery and the idea of natural superiority, it established the preservation of Catholicism, the sanctity of marriage, and the rights of children born "in" wedlock. Catholicism was made the state religion, and many revolutionary principles received the church's ostensible sanction.

Toussaint L'Ouverture considered himself to be a Frenchman and strove to convince Napoleon Bonaparte of his loyalty. Between the years 1800 and 1802, Toussaint L'Ouverture tried to rebuild the collapsed economy of Haiti and as an equal subject of France, reestablish commercial contacts with the United States and Britain.

Denying that he was trying to reinstate slavery, Napoleon sent his brother-in-law General Charles Le Clerc with thousands of troops and numerous warships to regain French control of the island in 1802.[10] Le Clerc landed on the island on January 20 and moved against Toussaint L'Ouverture. Four months later, on May 7, 1802, Toussaint L'Ouverture signed a treaty with the French in Cap-Haitien with the condition that there would be "no return to slavery." He retired to his farm in Ennery. After only three weeks, Le Clerc sent troops to seize Toussaint L'Ouverture and his family. Toussaint and his family were deported as captives to France on a warship reaching France on July 2. On August 25, 1802, Toussaint L'Ouverture was sent to Fort-de-Joux in Doubs where he was confined and repeatedly interrogated. While in prison, the "First of the Blacks" (Toussaint L'Ouverture) wrote to the "First of the Whites" (Napoleon Bonaparte) as defenders of fraternity, equality, and liberty. Giving testimony to his loyalty, he pleaded for just treatment. One of Toussaint's imprisonment declarations[11] stated:

> If I were to record the various services which I have rendered the Government, I should need many volumes, and even then should not finish them; and, as a reward for all these services, I have been arbitrarily arrested at St. Domingo, bound, and put on board ship like a criminal, without regard for my rank, without the least consideration. Is this the recompense due my labors? Should my conduct lead me to expect such treatment?

> I was once rich. At the time of the revolution, I was worth six hundred and forty-eight thousand francs. I spent it in the service of my country. I purchased but one small estate upon which to establish my wife and family. Today, notwithstanding my disinterestedness, they seek to cover me with opprobrium and infamy; I am made the most unhappy of men; my liberty is taken from me; I am separated from all that I hold dearest in the world,—from a venerable father, a hundred and five years old, who needs my assistance, from a dearly-loved wife, who, I fear, separated from me, can-

not endure the afflictions which overwhelm her, and from a cherished family, who made the happiness of my life.

On my arrival in France I wrote to the First Consul and to the Minister of Marine, giving them an account of my situation, and asking their assistance for my family and myself. Undoubtedly, they felt the justice of my request, and gave orders that what I asked should be furnished me. But, instead of this, I have received the old half-worn dress of a soldier, and shoes in the same condition. Did I need this humiliation added to my misfortune?

When I left the ship, I was put into a carriage. I hoped then that I was to be taken before a tribunal to give an account of my conduct, and to be judged. Far from it; without a moment's rest I was taken to a fort on the frontiers of the Republic, and confined in a frightful dungeon.

It is believed that Toussaint L'Ouverture never heard from Napoleon Bonaparte nor did he receive his moment before a tribunal. His letter, however, is revealing as to his consciousness. Until his death Toussaint had faith in France and considered himself to be an equal and loyal French subject. While in a French prison, the great Black liberator and loyal son of France died of pneumonia; and under the orders of the commander of the fort, was unceremoniously buried without a casket in a cave under the prison chapel.

A memetic analysis of Toussaint L'Ouverture is informative and revealing of his mind and consciousness. It is no small matter that Toussaint, though enslaved, grew up in a family of eight children headed by a native born African from Dahomey. His personal memetic ideation, which is probably typical of all the Africans of his generation, would have included cultural and familial ideas and beliefs passed on to him from his Arrada father that most likely included African ideas about spirit, respect for elders, personal responsibility, ancestor veneration, divine destiny, power of the word, justice in rulership (sovereignty), the nature of reality and the meaning of being human coming directly from Africa (Dahomey).

Toussaint's consciousness was also informed by his exposure to Catholicism, Greco-Roman thought, and the revolutionary writings of Abbé Raynal. His mental map included ideations reflecting beliefs in aristocracy, the denigration of Africa, class privilege, racial hierarchies, elitism, apostolic authority, patriarchal domination, caste (permanent attribution and place) and individualism. By his own declaration and even as a victim of French treachery, Toussaint believed in the French sense of being human. Toussaint's clarion call from the French prison at Fort-de-Joux in Doubs was an attempt to remind his captors that he was equal to them and obedient to their sense of privileged hierarchy (e.g., first amongst Blacks, Toussaint equal to first amongst Whites, Napoleon). This alone is clear evidence of his conflicted consciousness. For the French the new revolutionary ideas of fraternity, equality, and liberty stopped at the gates of color.

In addition to Francois Mackandal, Dutty Boukman, Cecile Fatiman, and Toussaint L'Ouverture, the other most notable leaders of the Haitian liberation struggles were Jacque Dessalines, Henry Christophe, and Alexandre Petion. Not only do these individuals represent the leadership that led to the establishment of the first independent Black nation in the Western hemisphere, they also give us a data set for further understanding the formation of Haiti's Cache of Consciousness.

With Toussaint L'Ouverture's ignoble betrayal and death, Haiti's "phantom of liberty"[12] and the establishment of "fraternity," "liberty" and "equality" was left to haunt "the three horsemen of Haiti's meme." Deeper analyses of their beliefs, as well as those of Mackandal, Boukman, and Fatiman, will help to illuminate the cache of memetic ideation reflective of the psycho-social and geopolitical consciousness represented by the Haitian mind.

Jean-Jacques Dessalines

Haiti's first "memetic horseman" was Jean Jacques Dessalines. He is said to have been born in Africa, most likely Guinea, around 1760 and brought to Saint Domingue by the French. His early life would have been nurtured by African memetic ideations tempered with invasion and possibly the experience of inter-tribal treachery and warfare. Dessalines was enslaved on a plantation in the northern province at Cormiers near the town of Grande-Reviere-du-nord. Sold to Henri Duckus, a French planter, Jean became a commandeur (slave foreman). For almost thirty years, Dessalines was "tormented" by the French. Dessalines was later resold around 1788 to a free Black man named Dessalines. It is said that he treated Jean and his two brothers very well. Jean and all his brothers adopted the surname of their Black owner.

Dessalines' story, like those of all great and small Black men, could not be completely told without speaking of the women in his life. One very important woman who had a significant influence in his early life was Victoria (Toya) Mantou. This African warrior woman taught Dessalines to be fearless; how to fight in hand-to-hand combat and to throw a knife. She was an extraordinary warrior, who commanded her own army and fought like her student, Dessalines, against the French in the Cahos Mountains of the Artibonite region. Dessalines' love and respect for her were unending. She lived as part of Emperor Dessalines' family until her death in 1805. The other significant woman, without whom there would have been no great liberator, was Marie-Claire Heureuse Félicité. Marie-Claire was born around 1758 and two years younger than Dessalines. She was said to have been the mistress of a planter who gave her a good education. In fact, C.L.R. James says that she was a woman of remarkable beauty, who was a healer and sympathetic to the French.[13] She was considered by her contemporaries as a "saint." It was during the battle of Jacmel that she first met Dessalines. It should be noted that Dessalines saw the French as his complete and forever enemy, who should be totally defeated and killed. In spite of his hatred for the French, Dessalines married his enemy's former mistress, and together they had a family and children (four daughters and three sons, including a pair of twins.) His love for her and the power of her humanity can only explain why Dessalines allowed her to bring aid and medicine to the injured of Jacmel. Dessalines' wife remained sympathetic to the French and saved the lives of many of them after independence. She died at the age of 100 in 1858.

Haiti's future liberator's life is also inextricably tied to another great Black woman, Marie-Jeanne Lamartiniere,[14] who was the African wife of one of Dessalines' mulatto commanders. The term mulatto requires some in text explanation. Its invention and usage are part of the language of oppression. Its use is itself a memetic infection. The etymology of the term, "mulatto[15]" is derived from the Spanish and Portuguese word, "mulato," which itself is derived from old Galician-Portuguese "mula" and Latin, "mūlusa," meaning the hybrid offspring of a horse and a donkey (i.e. mule). From the memetic ideation of the European enslavers, it was adopted to designate or classify the offspring resulting from the rape of African women and girls as if equivalent to donkeys. The use of this term was intentionally derogatory as an additional attempt to codify the degree of African inferiority. While in the United States, the one-drop rule (i.e., a single drop of Black blood made one Black and therefore inferior) prevailed, in Latin America, the Caribbean, and South America, especially in Brazil, the Dominican Republic, Cuba, and Puerto Rico, the mulatto thesis dominates.

At the siege of La Crete a Pierot, an epic struggle occurred that may have foretold the African victory in the struggle for freedom. The siege of La Crete is considered one of the great revolutionary epic battles of the war where Africans were outnumbered by the French 10 to 1. A little over a thousand Africans resisted 12,000 highly trained French troops, and history tells us that late at night on March 24, 1802, Marie-Jeanne was amongst the 1,200 besieged Blacks and so-called mulattos who cut and bayoneted their way through more than 10,000 French. Marie-Jeanne, who fought fiercely and valiantly, helped the Africans achieve an almost impossible escape that left many French generals and soldiers either dead or wounded. Marie-Jeanne Lamartiniere was pivotal in what was considered the most important battle of the Haitian Revolution and was personally honored by Dessalines[16] for her bravery.

Dessalines' personal history suggests a consciousness or mind map that included the recognition that one's "higher" status or rank, (i.e., commandeur-slave foreman) did not shield African people from the indignity found in the master-slave relationship.

Being a "commandeur," Dessalines did not command inviolable respect and honor. The memetic ideation that must have surrounded his mind was that of constant denigration and insecurity. He also experienced "good treatment" from his Black "owner" as evidenced by the fact that he and his brothers all adopted the free Black man's name of Dessalines. It was also under the "ownership" of this Dessalines that he was afforded the opportunity to court, fall in love, and marry Marie-Claire.

When Dessalines was about 31 years old, the Coachmen Conspiracy took place on the Leonard de Mezy Plantation, and the Bois Caimen ceremony led by Dutty Boukman and Cecile Fatiman took place in the northern province. Dessalines served as an officer in the French army when the colony was defending itself against Spanish and British incursions. He also fought under General Toussaint L'Ouverture against British and Spanish soldiers attempting to take the Haitian colony from France. Dessalines joined the rebellion started by Boukman and became a lieutenant in Papilon's forces. Following Toussaint's complex military stratagem, Dessalines, with the combined Black and mulatto forces, attacked and defeated the French forces under Rochambeau near Cap Francais in 1780 and rose to Brigadier General by 1799. It should be noted that Dessalines' military training was mostly at the hands of Black authority, e.g., Boukman, Toussaint, and Papilon. The memetic ideations embedded in his mental map due to these early military experiences were indeed complex. His consciousness would have included memetic ideations like, "whites were not invincible," "Blacks were worthy of leadership," "Blacks and mulattos had a common enemy," and above all, in this complexity of contradictory memetic ideations, the "love of Black people" was the ultimate determinant of one's decision making.

On December 4, 1803, Napoleon Bonaparte's French colonial army surrendered to Jean Jacques Dessalines' forces, resulting in the establishment of the world's first independent Black nation. He was a key leader of the Haitian Revolution and the first ruler of an independent Haiti under the 1801 constitution. Dessalines also believed in the strict regulation of foreign trade, which was essential for Haiti's sugar- and coffee-based export economy. He favored merchants from Britain and the United States over those from France. Clearly his early life experience created a consciousness that was informed by the experience of fighting for freedom under Black leadership (e.g., Toussaint and Papilon). His mental map included the critical ideation that the French were neither superior nor invincible.

For his administration, Dessalines needed literate and educated officials and managers. He placed, in these positions, well-educated Haitians who were disproportionately from the light-skinned elite. Having fought with both Black and mulatto revolutionaries, his consciousness was also informed by a perception, rightly or wrongly, that class differences were secondary to the love of Black people.

In September 1804, he proclaimed himself emperor. The following year Haiti's second constitution[17] was adopted. The language of this constitution is also very informative as to the consciousness or mind map of Dessalines and the revolutionaries who crafted it. The introduction that Christophe, Clerveaux, Petion, and others crafted reveals a memetic ideation that reflects a strong African sense of the Divine. They expressly assert that

> We… in our name as in that of the people of Hayti, who have legally constituted us faithfully organs and interpreters of their will, *in presence of the Supreme Being*, before whom all mankind are equal, and who has scattered so many species of creatures on the surface of the earth for the purpose of manifesting his glory and his power by the diversity of his works.[18]

The African memetic ideas embedded in this constitution are "God is omniscient and omnipresent (is in everything)," we are "instruments of divine will," and the "people are interdependent." Article 1 states that the people of Haiti have formed themselves into a free state sovereign and independent of any other power in the universe. Articles 2, 3, and 4 state that slavery is forever abolished; the Citizens of Hayti are brothers, equality in the eyes of the law is incontestably acknowledged, and there cannot be any titles, advantages, or privileges and that the law will be applied to all.

Articles 9, 10, 12 and 14 state that no person is worthy of being a Haitian who is not a good father, a good son, a good husband, and especially a good soldier; that fathers and mothers are not permitted to disinherit their children; that no white man of whatever nation he may be shall put his foot on this territory with the title of master or proprietor; and all Haytians shall hence forward be known only by the generic appellation of Blacks.

Regarding religion, the constitution states that the law admits of no predominant religion (Article 50); freedom of worship is tolerated (Article 51); and that the state will not provide for the maintenance of any religious institution (Article 52).

In struggling to establish the first independent Black nation in the Western Hemisphere, Dessalines was challenged with the need to stabilize the new nation state and to radically change the living conditions of the masses of the people. One of the provisions he established was designed to keep the people on the land where they could support themselves and not flee to the cities. This provision, however, kept the people in a condition that looked and felt no different from their previous enslavement and engendered the belief that he was forcing the newly freed back into slavery. However, as his system began to emerge, many Blacks fled into the hills to escape it.

Dessalines was assassinated two years after becoming the emperor of Haiti. It is believed that the conspiracy to overthrow Dessalines involved both Henri Christophe and Alexandre Pétion (who later did succeed him). He was assassinated near Port-au-Prince at a location called Pont Rouge (Red Bridge) on October 17, 1806, on his way to fight the rebels. However, given the fact that Christophe and Toussaint's sons helped to craft the constitution declaring Dessalines Emperor I of Hayti and Commander in Chief of the Army and in so doing swore to maintain the constitution that made Dessalines emperor to the last breath of his life, and the fact that Dessalines' nephew served as Christophe's personal assistant, field marshal, and third in command of the army, it is hard to reconcile without corroborating evidence that Christophe was involved with Dessalines' assassination. Yet, in light of the complexity of the memetic ideations constituting the consciousness of these revolutionaries' contradictory behaviors and beliefs, it is very possible.

Upon Dessalines' brutal assassination, with his body left on the Pont Rouge Bridge, Marie Sainte Dédée Bazile,[19] also called Défilée, gathered his remains and transported them to the Cimetière Intérieur (Interior Cemetery) of Port-au-Prince for a proper burial. She did not, however, just appear out of nowhere to bury Dessalines. Défilée was born near Le Cap where both her parents were enslaved and joined the revolution. Like many African women, she followed Dessalines' troops and alongside the men, gave support working as a peddler, soldier, spy, and in many instances, mother, daughter, and/or lover. According to the African belief in the afterlife and the importance of properly preparing the body for transitioning into the afterlife, it would not be far-fetched to recognize that this warrior woman gave Dessalines a proper burial after he was brutally assassinated and left to rot because such was required by African customs.

Henri Christophe

Haiti's second memetic horseman was Henri Christophe,[20] who was born in either Grenada or St. Christopher (St. Kitts) in the British Isles in 1767. The son of a freeman and an enslaved African woman, he was brought enslaved to Saint Domingue. At the age of 12, Christophe served as a drummer boy in the Chasseurs-Volontaires de Saint Domingue's Gens de Couleur regiment in the American Revolution in 1770. He fought at the Siege of Savannah. As an adult he worked as a mason, sailor, stable hand, waiter, billiard maker, and hotel restaurant manager in Cap Francais. Under these various conditions, it is said he was able to purchase his own freedom before the uprising of 1791.

Christophe was 24 when the Bois Caimen ceremony led by Boukman sparked the Haitian liberation struggle. Joining the uprising, he distinguished himself and rose to the rank of general in Toussaint L'Ouverture's army at the age of 25. A passage from Henri Christophe's personal secretary, who lived more than half his life enslaved, describes the crimes perpetrated against the Africans of Saint Domingue by the French:

> *Have they not hung up men with heads downward, drowned them in sacks, crucified them on planks, buried them alive, crushed them in mortars? Have they not forced them to consume feces? And, having flayed them with the lash, have they not cast them alive to be devoured by worms, or onto anthills, or lashed them to stakes in the swamp to be devoured by mosquitoes? Have they not thrown them into boiling cauldrons of cane syrup? Have they not put men and women inside barrels studded with spikes and rolled them down mountainsides into the abyss? Have they not consigned these miserable blacks to man eating-dogs until the latter, sated by human flesh, left the mangled victims to be finished off with bayonet and poniard?*[21]

After the French betrayed Toussaint L'Ouverture and attempted to re-establish slavery under Rochanbau, Christophe joined with Dessalines to defeat the French and establish Haiti as an independent Black nation.

With the unraveling of Haiti's nationhood and the assassination of Dessalines, Christophe was elected to the position of President of Haiti. However, with no real power and feeling both insulted and vulnerable to assassination, he retreated to the northern Provence and created a separate government declaring himself, "President and Generalissimo of the armies of the land and sea of the state of Haiti." Dessalines' nephew, Raymond Dessalines, served as "Marechal de Camp" (field marshal), third in command of the army and "aide de-camp" (personal assistant) to Henri Christophe when he was proclaimed Henri I, King of Haiti in 1811.

In 1811, Henri Christophe made the northern state a "kingdom" and was ordained by Arch Bishop of Milot Corneil Breuil as,

> *Henri, by the grace of God and the constitutional law of the state, King of Haiti, Sovereign of Tortuga, Gonave and*

*other adjacent islands, Destroyer of Tyranny, Regenerator
and Benefactor of the Haitian nation, Creator of her moral,
political and martial institutions, First crown and Monarch of
the new World, Defender of the faith, Founder of the Royal
Military Order of Saint Henry.*[22]

As King of Haiti, he renamed Cap Francais to Cap Henri;
established royalty in Haiti; and named his son Jacques-Victor
heir apparent with the title, Prince Royal of Haiti, all reflecting his
complicated consciousness. He created Haitian nobility (peerage)
with princes, dukes, counts, barons, and chevaliers. Christophe's
kingship was modeled, in part, after the "enlightened absolutism"
of Frederick the Great. He established a legal system called the
"Code of Henri," and although not formally educated, undertook
massive development projects. He created a theist school system,
supported the arts, and built magnificent edifices (six chateaus,
eight palaces, Sans Souci, and the massive Citadille LaFerriere).

The immediate intrigue concerning Christophe is recognition
that he was parented with ideas coming from his father who was
a "freeman" and his mother who was an "enslaved African." What
did he learn from his parents who were connected to a community
of memetic ideations? What beliefs, ideas, and values did they
instill in him? One could suggest that he may have learned from
his parents both the value and honor in being free, the constant
reminder of slavery, and the ever-present fear of losing one's
freedom. He would have had to internalize the African memetic
ideations of consubstantiation, humanness, propriety, and integrity.

From Christophe's early life as a drummer boy, mason, waiter,
sailor, and hotel manager, he was exposed to the social strata in
the white world. He witnessed first-hand not only how White people treated the Africans but also how they treated each other. The
memetic ideation embedded in his mental map shaped by exposure to the White world included aristocracy, place, class privilege,
racial categories, elitism, economic exploitation, theocracy, patriarchal domination, caste (permanent attribution), individualism, classism, and colorism. His mental map included ideations of regency,

security, the savagery and treachery of the French, importance of art and culture (European), and death before disgrace.

Having within his consciousness the Siege of Savannah (1779); the "alligator spark" (Bois Caimen Voodoo Ceremony), which ignited the Haitian revolution (1791), the betrayal of Toussaint (1802); the liberation of Haiti (1803); Haiti as a constitutional Empire (1804); the assassination of Dessalines (1806); and the establishment of a Haitian Kingdom in the northern state (1811), Christophe's mindset guided the governance of the first free Black republic with a complex and oftentimes conflicting cache of memetic ideations.

After ruling Haiti as King of Haiti, Sovereign of Tortuga, Gonave and other adjacent islands, destroyer of tyranny, regenerator and benefactor of the Haitian nation for almost a decade, Henri Christophe suffered a stroke in October 1820 that left him partially paralyzed. When the news spread of his infirmities, the conflicting consciousness and political interest representing the Haitian mindscape began to fester, and the seeds of rebellion began to grow.

On October 2, 1820, the military garrison at St. Marc led a mutiny that sparked a revolt. The mutiny coincided with a conspiracy of Christophe's own generals fed by their complicated and conflicting consciousness. Some of his trusted aides took him to the Citadel to await the inevitable confrontation with the rebels. Christophe ordered his attendants to bathe him and dress him in his formal military uniform, place him in his favorite chair in his den, and leave him alone. Shortly after the attendants left his side, Christophe committed suicide by shooting himself in the heart with a silver bullet. To prevent Christophe's body from being mutilated by the rebels, several of his aides buried him in quick lime.

Alexandre Sabes Petion

Haiti's third memetic horseman was Alexandre Sabes Petion. Alexandre Petion was born in 1770 as the son of a wealthy white father and a free born "Gens de Couleur" mother. At the age of 18, Alexandre was sent to France to be educated at the Military Academy in Paris. The Gens de Couleur represented a third or buffer class between the Gran and Petit Blancs (Whites) and the enslaved Africans (Blacks), who were also stratified as creoles (island born) and African born. An interesting fact is that before the uprising of 1791, the Gens de Couleur led a rebellion to gain voting and political rights they believed due them as French citizens after the French Revolution. At that time most did not support freedom or political rights for enslaved Africans and Blacks.[23] Returning to Saint Domingue, as a young military man, Alexandre participated in the creole expulsion of the British from Saint Domingue. However, tensions also grew between the Creoles and the Blacks. Symbolized by the "War of Knives" (Guerre des Couteaux), which was a nine-month (June 1799 to March 1800) conflict between the Blacks led by Toussaint L'Ouverture and the Mulattos led by Andre Rigaud.[24] In addition to the ongoing oppression and memetic ideational imposition by the Europeans, African unity on the island was eroded by memetic made tensions pitting Blacks and creoles against each other. Petion, true to his class, generally supported the mulatto factions. In a failed insurrection attempt against Toussaint, Petion, Ambre Rigaud, and Jean Pierre Boyer were exiled to France in 1800. Interestingly, Petion and the other exiled mulattos returned with Napoleon Bonaparte's brother-in-law, Charles Le Clerc, whose mission was to re-establish French control over Saint Domingue.

With Le Clerc's betrayal of Toussaint and his subsequent death and replacement by Rochambeau, Petion and the other Mulatto leaders realized that France's real mission was genocide, so they joined forces with the Africans under the leadership of Jean Jacques Dessalines. After the assassination of Dessalines, the country became divided with the north being ruled as a royal kingdom under Henri Christophe and the south remaining a Republic under the direction of Alexandre Petion, a Gens de Couleur. Simon Bolivar, in his own independence struggle against Spain, sought refuge in Haiti, and under the condition that he free any enslaved Africans he encountered in his fight for South American freedom, Petion provided Simon Bolivar with soldiers, weapons, and financial assistance to help liberate Venezuela.

Alexandre Petion was succeeded by Jean Pierre Boyer, also a "homme de couleur," who reunified the island and freed the Africans still in captivity in Saint Domingue. He also attempted to save the struggling economy by establishing the "Code Rural," which tied the newly freed to their former plantations and prevented them from entering the towns or starting farms or independent businesses of their own. In effect, he knowingly or unknowingly created a policy that resulted in a kind of re-enslavement.

When France's King Charles X sent a fleet of 14 war vessels and thousands of troops to Haiti in an attempt to shatter Haiti's fragile independence, Boyer, under pressure, agreed to a treaty wherein France would formally recognize Haiti's independence in exchange for a payment of 150 million francs as an indemnity for losing to the Blacks and profits lost from the trade in captive human beings. The complex conflicting cache of Haitian consciousness may help to explain why Boyer could believe that paying France an indemnity for losing to the Haitians somehow made good sense.

Haitian consciousness has been fed by the seeds of this cache of consciousness found in the mental maps of the architects of the revolution. The retention of European (French) memetic ideations found in Haitian consciousness were ideas and beliefs reflecting African denigration and supportive of a European worldview which privileged whiteness, particularly Frenchness, and demeaned the value of anything African, including African independence.

The memetic ideation of the Code Noir essentially codified the European memetic cluster and created law, which resulted in a symbiotic infection of African consciousness. This infected African consciousness included memetic ideations that supported behaviors that reinforced and/or propagated "whiteness" (Frenchness) as sensate soria, having the attributes of sacred, superior, authoritative, accountable, and that white people (1) had power over life and death and (2) that being civilized was equal to being White (French).

The retention of African memetic ideations was also found in Haitian consciousness. Memetic ideations of the power of spirit, respect for elders, personal responsibility, ancestor veneration, divine destiny, power of the word, and just and morally right ruler-ship were retentions of African beliefs. Equally present within Afri-can ideations was the nature of reality and the meaning of being human as spirit, energy, or power as well as the belief that human beings are instruments of divine will and that people are interde-pendent. This complex of memetic ideations is all found in Haitian consciousness.

The hermeneutics of consciousness, in a sense, determine or allow African people to conceive of and understand themselves as fundamentally spirit. From an African worldview, consciousness is thought to be intricately merged with spirit. It is the "knowing" of what a knowing and knowable spirit knows. All that is conscious-ness is, in fact, revealed in and determined by energy in motion (relationships). At the most fundamental level, consciousness is found in the "pulse" that gives us life. In contestation to a Euro-pean worldview and consciousness, consciousness relative to African people should be thought of as a construct that represents the ability of human beings to know, perceive, understand, and be aware of self in relation to self and all else. Uncontaminated Hai-tian consciousness should, therefore, be viewed as an example of African consciousness in the form of awareness, knowing, com-prehension, and existence (being).

Equally embedded in Haitian consciousness is an African me-metic ideation which results in a symbiotic infection of the Haitian mind so as to support behaviors that reinforce and propagate beliefs in a deeper meaning in everything. Spirit is essential and is seen as a powerful invisible process that influences behavior. Living ancestral spirits are believed to continue to be involved with the living and are capable of utilizing the invisible (mysteries). These African memetic ideations served as the nurturing seeds of the Haitian complex of conflicting consciousness. This cache is both the template and prototype of the Haitian mind, a mind that in a complex and almost perverse way loves everything Haitian but Haitians.

The contemporary disconnection from African sense of consciousness was and remains the intent and consequence of Eurocentric intellectual (conceptual) hegemony and worldwide White (political and philosophical) supremacy. It is clear that the "remembering" or "re-experiencing" of an African meaning of consciousness is essential to the liberation of the African mind and the development, empowerment, and revitalization of African people worldwide. The vibratory events known as the Haitian revolution must be interpreted or illuminated as psychological phenomena. This is the hidden and most often misunderstood significance of Voodoo for Haitian consciousness.

---

[1] Consciousness, as conceived by African people, is, in effect, a construct that represents the ability of human beings to know, perceive, understand, and be aware of self in relation to self and everything else. It is the hermeneutics of consciousness that determines how African people conceive of and understand themselves as fundamentally spirit. This awareness of one's self as spirit, in turn, allows one to access realms of knowing that are not limited to just cognition or perception. It also allows one to be accessible to those spirits in the realm of the spirit. It connects knowing and awareness to both the perceivable (visible) and the unperceivable (invisible). Hence, consciousness is not bound by time, space, or place. It connects knowing, awareness, and comprehension to the universal and the Divine. Consciousness is that which gives congruity among the various realms of being. See *Shattered Consciousness and Fractured Identity: The Lingering Psychological Effects of the Transatlantic Slave Trade Experience* (2008) by Wade Nobles.

[2] From Fu-Kiau, K. (2001, pp. 17-22). *Tying the Spiritual Knot: African Cosmology of the Bantu-Kongo.*

[3] Fu-Kiau, K. (2001, pp. 22-40).

[4] Higgins, C. (1994). *Feeling the Spirit: Searching the World for the People of Africa.*

[5] See Rainsford, M. (1805). *An Historical Account of the Black Empire of Hayti: Comprehending a View of the Principal Transactions in the Revolution of Saint Domingo.*

[6] See Geggus, D. (2002). *Haitian Revolutionary Studies.*

[7] See Baptiste, S. & Relly, J.R. (1863). *Toussaint L'Ouverture: A Biography and Autobiography.*

[8] Madam Toussaint weighed 250 pounds when she was captured, and upon her release she weighed less than 90 pounds. She died at the age of 67 in Jamaica in 1846.

[9] Constitution of Haiti (1801), (M. Abidor Trans.) (See Appendix 2).

[10] History of Haiti retrieved from http://library.brown.edu/haitihistory/9.html.

[11] See Baptiste, S. & Relly, J.R. (1863). *Toussaint L'Ouverture: A Biography and Autobiography.*

[12] See Carruthers, J. (1985). *The Irritated genie: An essay on the Haitian revolution.*

[13] See James, C.L.R. (1989). *The Black Jacobins.*

[14] Marie-Jeanne Lamartiniere fought valiantly alongside Dessalines at the siege of La Crete a Perot.

[15] Barnhart, R. (2003, p. 684). *Chambers Dictionary of Etymology.*

[16] History is unclear as to the timing and accuracy of Dessalines' relation to another woman of the Haitian revolution. It is said that Sanita Belaire was equivalent to a sergeant in Toussaint L'Ouverture's revolutionary forces when she, along with her husband, Charles Belaire (Toussaint's nephew), were executed (October 5, 1802) by a French firing squad under the command of Dessalines, who at that time was serving the French army. The reported timing of this would have been seven months after Dessalines was assisted by the African woman, Marie-Jeanne Lamartiniere, at the siege of La Crete a Perot. It seems improbable that Dessalines would have been working for the French in October when he was in a struggle to the death against the French in March or that he would have ordered the execution of an African woman and the nephew of Toussaint when his very life was saved by the heroism of another African woman.

[17] The Second Constitution of Haiti (Hayti), May 20, 1805, promulgated by Emperor Jacques I Dessalines. The document was printed in the *New York Evening Post*, July 15, 1805. (See Appendix 3).

[18] Constitution of Haiti (Hayti),

[19] See Philippe R. Girard's *The Slaves Who Defeated Napoleon: Toussaint L'Ouverture and the Haitian War of Independence, 1801-1804* (2011) for a discussion of the role of women in the revolution.

[20] See C.L.R. James' *The Black Jacobins* (1968) for a classic discussion of the Haitian revolution and Walter Monfried's "The Slave Who Became King: Henri Christophe" (Negro Digest, October 1963) for an in-depth discussion of the reign of Henry Christophe.

[21] Henri Christophe's personal secretary.

[22] Clive, C. (2007). *The Armorial of Haiti: Symbols of Nobility in the Reign of Henry Christophe.*

Chapter Six

Tornadoes of the Mind: Revisiting the Unfinished Revolution

"And you know, Kristi, something happened a long time ago in Haiti, and people might not want to talk about it. They were under the heel of the French, you know, Napoleon the Third and whatever, and they got together and swore a pact to the devil. They said, 'We will serve you if you'll get us free from the French.' True story. And so the devil said, 'O.K., it's a deal.'"

This final chapter begins with a quote from the "memetically infected" televangelist Pat Robertson.[1] His thoughts typify the hidden underbelly of most people's perception of the core African spiritual system found throughout the African world, especially in Haiti. The question of Haiti's restoration is, for Robertson and others, inextricably connected to the need to de-Africanize and demonize Haiti's retention of its African spiritual system (i.e., Vodou). What has come to be known as Voodoo in Haiti, and the ongoing need to eliminate Haiti's retention of it, has served as the hidden litmus test, ergo, the rejection or denial of Haiti's acceptance into the "modern" world of free and independent nations.

In effect, the lingering psychological effect of the Trans-Atlantic Slave Trade in Africans has been the continuous and constant assault and redefining of the African sense of being human and African. The result of this situation is defined as the shattering of consciousness and fracturing of identity. Shattered consciousness and fractured identity have resulted in a state of "spirit damage," which limits, curtails, and contains the African's capacity to be a full knowing and knowable unfolding spirit capable of achieving a never-ending totality of possibilities emerging from the African diaspora's ever-expanding perceivable and unperceivable multiverse. Restoration of shattered consciousness and shattered identity must be the central impetus in Haiti's recovery.

When one's consciousness is shattered, identity fractured, and self (person) alienated, distorted, or violated, the result causes a disability or malfunctioning that extends into and affects (however, subtly) each and every other self (person) in the community.

What is even more profound is that the "sickness" (weakness) or "health" (strength) of past generations also extends into and affects those who are alive today. The trauma of past enslavement extends into each of their descendants.

The retention of European (French) memetic ideations found in Haitian consciousness was ideas and beliefs supportive of aristocracy and class privilege. It also included inherited role status (hierarchies), elitism, subjugation, life-long slavery, racial/genetic inferiority, hierarchies, apostolic authority, exaltation of Christ and Christianity, and "whiteness," particularly Frenchness (viewed as sacred, superior, and powerful). To be civilized was, in deed and image, equaled to White (French), denigration of Africa, class privilege, patriarchal domination, caste (permanent attribution and place), and individualism. The Haitian was "civilized" to respect only European ownership of land and people; sanctioned acclimation to enslavement, acceptance of capricious evil acts as normal punishment (from rape to family separation to killings), personal inferiority, and the perpetuation of social distinctions.

The memetic ideation of the Code Noir essentially codified and in some ways calcified the European (French) mindset through the creation of laws, which resulted in a symbiotic infection of African consciousness. These codes served to support behaviors that reinforced and/or propagated "whiteness" (Frenchness) as sensate soria having the attributes of being sacred, superior, authoritative, and omnipotent and having power over life and death.

In understanding Haiti's Cache of Consciousness, one has to also examine the African memetic cluster that constitutes the Haitian consciousness and mindset. The assaulted Africans of then Saint Domingue were primarily Dahomians, Igbo, Nago, Hausa, Aja, Ewe, and Fon from West Africa (currently, Benin, Togo, and Nigeria) and BaKongo and Mandingo from Central Africa (currently, Angola and Kongo).[2] These West and Central Africans all carried beliefs (memetic clusters) in, for example, spirit beings who protect and guide the lives of the living. The memetic ideation of the ancient Fon Vodu, later to become Haitian Voodoo, was grounded on the BaNtu-Kongo belief that diverse forces and waves of energy govern life surrounding humans. The fire-force called Kalunga is complete in and of itself and emerges within the emptiness or nothingness and becomes the source of life on earth. The BaNtu-Kongo believe that the heated force of Kalunga blew up and down as a huge storm of projectiles, *Kimbwandende*, producing a huge mass in fusion. To explain the creation of the earth, the BaNtu describe the earth's formation as the cooling of the fire-force Kalunga and the fusion of the mass emptiness into a solid form, which represented the birth of the earth.[3]

In effect, as noted in Chapter Four, the BaNtu believe that all of reality (Kalunga) is fundamentally a process of perpetual and mutual sending and receiving of spirit (energy) in the form of waves and radiations. Kalunga or reality is the totality, the completeness of all life. It is an ocean of energy, a force in motion. Kalunga is everything, sharing life and becoming life continually after life itself. As the totality or the complete living, Kalunga is comprised of both a visible realm (Ku Nseke) and an invisible realm (Ku Mpemba). The visible physical world has spirit (energy) as its most important element. Referred to as Nkisi (medicine), the spirit element of the physical (visible) world has the power to care, cure, heal, and guide. The invisible (spiritual) world (Ku Mpemba) is comprised of human experience, ancestor experience, and the soul-mind experience. The Ku Mpemba has spirit (energy) as its most important element. In effect, if reality (visible and invisible) is, it is spirit. BaNtu-Kongo thought is, therefore, essential to our understanding of African sensorial-information structures and emblematic symbolism.

The Fon, Ayizi, Aja, and Evhe, from Benin (ancient Dahomey), carried in their consciousness the idea of "Bo" (power or energy) and "Bocio" meaning empowered and body, respectively. Combined, these two ideations gave birth to a belief in or ideation of empowered spirit-body (gods in the earth—little forest spirits (Aziza), fetishes, and orisas) having the "power to activate," protect, and direct human affairs.[4] The idea of "Bo" also constituted a "memetic ideation" of the sacredness of life, time, and locale. Psychologically, or in terms of consciousness, the "Bo" gave credence to or directed and encouraged Africans, now in Haiti, to understand and utilize that which is invisible in the visible. It guided and/or represented the potentiality of Haitian action to uncover the hidden potentiality of all things.

The retention of African memetic ideations is key to understanding Haitian and all diasporan African consciousness. African memetic ideations include the power of spirit, respect for elders, personal responsibility, ancestor veneration, divine destiny, power of the word, just sovereignty, the nature of reality, and the meaning of being human as spirit, energy, or power. They provide a consciousness that recognized that human beings are "instruments of divine will" and "people are interdependent." It is what drove the Haitian revolutionaries to encode constitutional ideas like "slavery is forever abolished," "the Citizens of Hayti are all brothers," and "Haiti was a free state sovereign and independent of any other power in the universe," "no white man of whatever nation he may be, shall put his foot on this territory with the title of master or proprietor," and "all Haytians shall hence forward be known only by the generic appellation of Blacks."[5]

Equally so, African memetic ideations resulted in a symbiotic infection of Haitian consciousness so as to support behaviors that reinforced and propagated beliefs in a deeper meaning in everything. Spirit is essential; it is a powerful invisible process that influences behavior. Living ancestral spirits continue to be involved with the living and are capable of utilizing the invisible (mysteries). African memetic ideations also served as the nurturing seeds of the Haitian Cache of Consciousness.

A full and accurate understanding of any African experience must be obtained using African language and logic. This idea seems to be in the form of a simple statement, but in actuality, the colonization of the African mind has been so pervasive that the idea of an African logic is almost imperceptible and incomprehensible. Nevertheless, it is believed that a total appreciation of the African experience, especially its Haitian expression, is only attainable through the prism of African logic and language.

The "psycho – logic" of the Kongo people, who are one of the founding strands making up the African captives of Hispaniola, asserts a belief or the idea that an inner divine presence (kingongo) is in harmony (blends) with the Ngulo, which is an "energy of self-healing power."[6] Ngulo is therein embedded in every and all forms of being. Accordingly, "Spirit well-being" is when the community's "inner divine presence" (Kingongo) is in harmony. That is to say, the inner divine presence of the members of the community is in harmony with the inner divine presence of others as well as the Ngulo as expressed as other living beings (i.e., trees, animals, land, water, air, etc.). Kingongo "psycho – logic" confirms that the laws of community life must be aligned with Divine law.

However, when members of the community violate or have violated the sacredness of their Kingongo, a condition called Sumuna happens. Sumuna is caused directly by the breaking of taboos, cultural precepts, and ancestral traditions. Any human relations, especially those that demean, denigrate, and dehumanize, that violate the sacred inner self result in Sumuna. Sumuna, in turn, creates a condition called "Kizungu Zongu," which is akin to "tornadoes of the mind" or a form of insanity. "Kizungu Zongu" is grounded in the idea or recognition that the laws of community life must be aligned with Divine law. When a person or community's self-sacredness is violated, the act or actions create "Kizungu Zongu" (tornadoes of the mind). In this circumstance, the individual or community is thought to have metaphorically turned or was forced to turn their backs against their own essence (sacredness within them), which should be thought of as spirit defilement.[7]

The idea of "tornadoes of the mind" or "Kizungu Zongu" can be thought of as "Traumatized Disconnected Spirit" (TDS), which presents itself as a syndrome of psychological inadequacy and limitation relative to consciousness and identity. As a consequence of enslavement and colonization, TDS can be seen almost everywhere Africans have experienced white supremacy masked as westernization, especially the United States, Haiti, Cuba, Brazil, and South Africa.

Haiti is a country created in 1804 by Africans kidnapped and stolen from West Africa at a time when slavery still flourished in the United States, South America, and other parts of the Caribbean. The sovereignty of Haiti, however, was not recognized either by the Roman Catholic Church or by nations that controlled trade across the Atlantic, including the United States, France, and Spain. For claiming their freedom and initially attempting to reject the cruel mentality of Western thought, particularly that of the French, Haiti has been punished ever since by the French who, in the 1820s, demanded and received reparations for the damage caused to France by Africans freeing themselves, which, in part, significantly impoverished Haiti at the very time of its birth.[8] Haiti was further assaulted by a brutal and savage American occupation from 1915 to 1934 that established and encouraged an indigenous misrule abetted by the American government. This set of events led to a geo-political and socio-economic legacy that continues to this day with American administrations engaging in a pattern of promoting and then undermining Haitian constitutional democracy.

Shattered Diasporan Consciousness

The more subtle and sublime damage found in Haiti's Cache of Consciousness is, however, harder to detect and is almost invisible. Nevertheless, it is at the heart of the syndrome of a traumatized disconnected spirit in the human family. The direct evidence of disconnected spirit is the limiting of one's humanity to a racial category defined by racism. In this regard, the structure of disconnected spirit takes form as an eroding expression that is so subtle it was often misperceived and/or misunderstood as almost normal. First and most damaging is that disconnected spirit causes Black people to deny or claim as irrelevant anything African as having value and worth in the conduct of life and living. When addressing or confronting the big questions or challenges of living, this syndrome inhibits African people from ever even considering that African thought or beliefs may have value in solving the problems of human life.

Unfortunately, the phenomena of shattered African consciousness and fractured Black identity are not just unique to Haiti. It is symptomatic of contact with White people and their worldview, which supports, if not requires, the dehumanization and de-Africanization of the African. There is evidence of these phenomena throughout the African diaspora as well as throughout the continent of African itself.

In Cuba, for instance, little that is Cuban can, in fact, be divorced from its largely African roots.[9] Yet Cuba today has been structured to intentionally eliminate "racism" without clarifying the distinction between racist beliefs and customs and the cultural integrity of the people victimized by racism. The history of racism is a complex issue for the revolution. For example, in understanding the issue of racism in Cuba, one must minimally distinguish between the interest of the Spanish (oppressor) and the agency of the African (oppressed). Yet most analyses only speak to or through the "voice" (memetic ideation) of the dominating class. For example, what did the slave owning class do to the enslaved rather than what did the enslaved do to protect and project their own humanity? Many scholars attempt to understand the Cuban experience by noting that the landowning and slave owning classes of Cuba, because they feared Spain's possible capitulation to Britain's pressure to end the slave trade, opted for annexing Cuba into the United States.

The so-called reformists, who were staunch defenders of slavery, only wanted to renegotiate the colonial relationship with Spain so as to ensure Cuba's greater profit and benefit. In this vein, the reformists established a cynical policy that divided Black people into Blacks and so-called Mulattos (memetic ideation) and gave the so-called mulattos special privileges, especially the gift of possible assimilation (a meme) as a means of gaining allies. The possibility of "blanqueamiento" or "whitening" (memetic ideation), which resulted in Black people wanting to transform themselves into so-called mulattos and the so-called mulattos evolving into white people, has so complicated the question of racism, race relations, and the quest for human integrity that scholarship on the presence and importance of African people as Africans has been rendered irrelevant and/or impossible. But what did the Africans actually do in response to this psychological terrorism? For example, seventy percent of the members of the independence army of 1868 were Black people (even though some were defined as so-called mulattos).[10] Yet the role, influence, and understandings of African consciousness of Black revolutionary leaders like Antonio and Jose Maceo, Guillermon Moncado, Flor Crombet and Quintin Bandera on Cuba's development has not been fully understood or explored.

Many Afro-Cuban thinkers have suggested that in many ways Cuba's history has been rewritten using the ink of "blanqueamiento."[11] It is noted for instance that Danzon,[12] the historical dance of Black people that was viewed as evidence of savagery, has now gained respectability as the national (Cuban, ergo white) dance form. African religions (Abakua and Nago), which actually played crucial roles in the formation of Cuba's revolution and nationhood, were transformed into witchcraft and ignorant superstition and later retransformed into cultural exotica in the service of today's emerging White tourist industry. The African cultural renaissance of the 1930s with the Afrocentric poetry of Nicolas Guillen and Zacarias Tallet, the anthropological and ethnological research of Fernando Ortiz, the acknowledged African rhythms and melodies of Amadeo Roldan, Alejandron Garcia Caturla and Ernesto Lecuana; the popular "sones" of Miguel Metramoro and Sando Garay, and the paintings of Abela, Victor Manual, Amelia Palaez, Wilfredo Lam, and Portocarrero all reflect the Africa within Cuba's soul[13] and clearly reveal the African foundation of Cuba's voice. Yet the African nature of this history is slowly disappearing (being overtaken by non-African memetic ideations.) The triumph of the Cuban revolution, led by the young attorney Fidel Castro Ruiz, in actuality benefitted from the long struggle for liberty and justice waged by primarily Afro-Cubans for almost a century. Ironically Black revolutionaries have rationalized that the goal of the revolution was so laudable that they were and are willing to overlook Cuba's persistent racism in support of the revolution. Hence, the continuous cancer of "blanqueamiento" continues.

Shattered consciousness and fractured identity in Mexico is another example of blanqueamiento. While many Mexican intellectuals, like 20th century philosopher Jose Vasconcelos, claimed to support the desire to create a "cosmic race" by mixing the races into a single homogeneous form. The obvious intent was to eliminate the African and indigenous (Indian) forms. All the racial categories (e.g., Mestizo, so-called Mulatto, Negro, Negros Atezados, very dark Black people; and Negros retintos, double-dyed Black people) were created to serve the idea of Mejorar La Raza (improving the race). Africa's presence in Mexico[14] is often denied. Mexico, like other Latin American countries, identifies itself as a nation of "Mestizos," people of mixed Indian and Spanish blood. There, in fact, is no or little official acceptance of the African ethnic and cultural elements in the national heritage or consciousness of Mexico. To the contrary, these elements are denigrated and dismissed.

While the negative memetic ideation regarding Black people is found in the saying, "Los Negros son solo los Burros; nosotros somos prietos" (Negroes are donkeys; we are dark), Afro-Mexican people have influenced almost every aspect of Mexican life, culture, and history. In spite of it being denied, Mexico is significantly African. Black people were critical to the early development of Mexico's economy and played a leading role in the war for independence. A Moor named Esteban el Negro (Steven the Black) explored Northern Mexico, including Texas and New Mexico. El Negro also founded the legendary city of Cibola. Africans made important contributions to Mexico's folktales, religion, medicinal practices, cooking styles, music, and dance. The song "La Bamba," popularized in the 60s by the group Los Lobos, was in fact, sung as early as 1683 by Black people in Veracruz.[15] Bamba is also a traditional dance.[16] The word Bamba or Mbamba is the name of an ethnic group in Angola. Traditional Mexican music, in fact, finds a significant part of its origins in Mexico's blackness. The popular sones like La Morena, La Negra, and El Maracumbe are stylistically African music forms. The Mexican dances like the "Jarabe," "Chillina," "Gusto," and "Zapateo" were all created by Afro-Mexicans. The "Corrido," a narration in the first and third person by a "Corridista," is usually recited or sung in a so-called Afro-Mexican dialect. The dialect or language of the Afro-Mexican is, not surprisingly, said to be "unintelligible Spanish".[17] What is probably more accurate is that what is called Afro-Mexican dialect is Afro-Mexicans speaking Spanish using African linguistic rule structures, ergo, Spanish Ebonics.

Many historically Black communities along the Atlantic coast of Mexico bear truth to the African presence in Mexico. Coastal towns called Angola, Guinea, Mozambique, and Cerro del Congo (names of African countries/peoples) and settlements named in recognition of the ethnic groups who came to Mexico, like La Mandigo, El Mocambo, La Matanba, and El Monzonga, all testify to the African presence in Mexico. The towns of San Lorenzo de los Negros (later named "Yanga" after the Black Liberation fighter) and Mandinga y Matosa (named after the maroon leader Francisco de la Matosa) were named in honor of major African personalities in Mexico.[18]

It is estimated that between the coming of Hernan Cortez in 1519 and the start of Mexico's war for independence in 1810, more than a half million Africans were brought into Mexico. In the late 16th and 17th centuries, Mexico enslaved more Africans than any other country in the Americas. Additionally, "Ladinos" (Africans born and Hispanized in the Caribbean, Spain, or Portugal) continued to enter Mexico through the ports of Acapulco, Veracruz, Campeche, and Panuco. According to the writer Aguirre Beltran, in the 16th century, Afro-Mexicans constituted 71 percent of the non-indigenous population. By the 18th century, the number of Afro-Mexicans had decreased to about 65 percent. In the 16th century, the main cause of death for the Afro-Mexican population was European diseases, particularly yellow fever, tuberculosis, and syphilis. While decreases in the population due to these diseases and those caused by working in the sugar cane fields and the silver mines are given as reasons for the decrease in the Afro-Mexican population, another reason for the decrease in African people in Mexico can be attributed to the "Whitening of the race"

(Blanqueamiento). In Mexico, it was legally and socially beneficial for Afro-Mexicans to mix with either the indigenous people or the Spanish. Black women who married Hispanic men, in fact, "improved" their social status and that of their children.

However, Africans and so-called mulattos, at the hands of the Spanish, were perceived in negative ways (negative African memetic ideations) and were brutally oppressed both physically and psychologically. The Spanish memetic ideations described the Africans as "vicious people," "naturally evil," of a "bad race," "bellicose," and "bestial." The offspring of the African and indigenous people were known as Jaruco (wild pig), Chino, or lobo (wolf). In the 17th century, the Spanish established a social system based on an elaborate color bar (memetic ideation) that controlled every aspect of life for Afro-Mexicans. Every person of African or indigenous ancestry was denied rights to education and was not allowed to bear arms, to travel freely at night, to wear jewelry or silk, or to even marry without permission. For those violating these laws, the punishment was as excessive and brutal as castration, maiming, and disfigurement. It is clear that these social conventions (memetic ideations) were invented, internalized, and designed to de-Africanize the Afro-Mexicans. These and other injustices led many Afro-Mexicans to escape to "Palenques" (armed settlements of escaped Africans) where Afro-Mexicans could live as free and African. The best-known "Palenque," Yanga, is still in existence.

In Mexico, Black revolutionaries connected the war for independence from Spain with the emancipation of enslaved Africans. Afro-Mexicans like El Negro Guerrero (Vincente Guerrero), who later became Mexico's second President, Juan del Carmen, Juan Bautista, Francisco Gomez, and Jose Maria Alegra, as well as General Jose Maria Moreles, all played significant roles in the winning of Mexico's independence from Spain. Some historians point out that it was in fact, the "ejércita morena" (dark army) of Father Hidalgo that actually launched the independence struggles in Mexico. Ironically, or unfortunately, in reaction to Spanish racism, El Negro Guerrero and other Black revolutionaries wanted all the people of the new nation to think in terms of nationality and not race. The idea of "Mejorar la Raza" was to mix the races to form a homogenous group and in so doing dilute the African ancestry and create a better homogenous "La Raza Cosmínica" (cosmic race). Those who had been referred to (and ill-treated), by the Spanish as Mestizo, so-called mulatto, Negro, and Indio now demanded to be simply called Mexican (memetic ideation). After independence, children were recorded as Mexican rather than Negro or Indio, etc. However, given the legacy of Spain, to be African or Indio was to be in the most undesirable position (memetic ideation), and many Afro-Mexicans tried to "pass" the color line into the status of Criollo (a white person of Spanish origin) if possible (if light enough) or, if not so lucky, to be amongst the indigenous (the proverbial, "I got a little Indian in me.") Unfortunately, since the beginning of Spanish domination and corruption (Spanish memetic imposition) in Mexico, people of African ancestry have been portrayed and defined in a litany of inferior and negative images and stereotypes. The popular Mexican saying, *"Trabaja duro como un Negro para vivir como un Blanco"* (Work hard like a Nigger to live like a White),[19] speaks volumes to the shattered African consciousness and fractured Black identity.

While many, if not most, Mexicans will boast of their Spanish heritage or relatives (the lingering memetic ideation supporting de-Africanization in Mexico), rarely will one admit to having a Black grandparent or invest their time in finding common ground with other Africans in the Americas. Hence, as a direct consequence of this psychological warfare, many Afro-Mexicans moved and continue to move further away from their African identity.

The social construction of the Mexican identity with a national consciousness about being African was driven by notions or ideas like Mestizo, Criollo, Blanqueamiento, la Raza, Blanquitos, Morenos, so-called mulattos, Negros Puros, and Cuculustes. However, alongside this socially constructed national heritage, the lives and presence of the likes of Esteban el Negro, Diego Rivera, El Negro Guerrero, Ejercita Morena, Yanga, and Francisco de la Matosa made the Mexican non-African national heritage a lie. Additionally, the undeniable African cultural forms of La Bamba, La Morena, La

Negra, El Maracumbe, Jarabe, Chilena, Gusto, Zapateo and Corrido serve as evidence of Mexico's complex cache of identity.
Brazil, not usually referred to as Latin, with its nearly 50 percent African population, represents yet another location for examining shattered African consciousness and fractured Black identity.
The free African community (Maroon society) that operated as an
independent African-centered state for nearly two centuries serves
as an historical reservoir for authenticating African cultural and political survivals in the Americas. Within Afro-Brazil there is source
material for documenting the African character of warfare and new
world religions (e.g., Candomblè), music and dance (Mambo,
Samba, Bossa Nova, Ngola, Capoeira et al.) Understanding the
Brazilian government's two-fold strategy of racial miscegenation for
the purpose of "whitening" its citizenry and the prohibition of black
immigration, while encouraging white immigration, serves to
illuminate the cache of Afro-Brazilian consciousness. The perverse
strategy was and remains another variation on the Brazilian col-
loquialism, *"Branca para casar, Negra p'ra trabalhar Mulata p'ra
fornicar"*[20] (White women for marrying, Black women for work,and
Mulatto women for fornication).This strategy is well documented in
the book *Brazil, Mixture or Massacre* by one of Brazil's most famous Afro-Brazilian activists, Abdias Do Nascimento. Like Mexico
and Cuba, the African presence and contributions to Brazilian life
were critical to the actual formation of the development of the nation. Yet African phenomena is strangely denied or mutated by the
psychological assault in Brazil called "embranquecimento" (whitening). The African experience in Brazil has been literally shaped by
an overt attempt to eliminate the sense of being African. The idea of
Embranquecimento (the whitening of the race or more accurately the elimination of the African) became the official priority
in Brazil in the1850s.[21] As a continuous legacy of the memetic infection of embranquecimento (whitening), according to the 1980s
census, Brazilians had coined 136 different terms of racial catego-
rization. Starting with the 19th century novelist Jose Maria Mach-
ado de Asis and continuing on to the present day, members of the
Brazilian so-called Mulatto class have been diabolically awarded

better living conditions and respect.[22] In addition to Embranqueci-mento, Brazil's whitening process systematically gave, and still gives, greater respect and value to Morenidade (Brunettism) as a valued objective in its historical race mixing for social betterment. What, therefore, does it mean for African people to be subjected to the message of "embranquecimento"?

In the context of the Afro-Brazilian experience, one must discuss the purpose of "embranquecimento" (whitening) and Afro-Brazilian response and reaction to being "whitened."[23] A partial historical timeline of Brazil is informative. The Portuguese occupa-tion of Brazil began in 1500, and some 3.6 million Africans were brought into Brazil.[24] In 1625 Brazil witnessed the establishment of the Quilombos and the spirit of the Zumbi. In 1792 Joaquim Jose da Silva Xavier Tiradentes led one of the earlier independence movements, and the Portuguese Court condemned him to death by hanging. Six years later, the Sastre Rebellion (1798) occurred in Bahia where the majority of the enslaved Africans were held. In response to Napoleon's threat to invade and conquer Portugal, the Portuguese Court was transferred to Brazil. The court ruled from Brazil from 1808-1821. During the same period and more (1807-1835), Africans constantly rebelled against their enslavement and continually waged liberation struggles/battles against the Portu-guese. Major liberation battles were waged by Muslim Africans almost every other year (1810, 1813, and 1816) during the occu-pation of the Portuguese Court.[25]

In 1821, King Dom Juan VI returned to Portugal and left his son Dom Pedro I to rule Brazil. Is it possible that the Africans made Brazil too difficult or too dangerous for the King of Portugal? A year after his father's departure, Dom Pedro I proclaimed Bra-zil's independence from Portugal. Four years later (1825), Brazil witnessed the Jihad and the Black Nagos' war of liberation from 1826-1835. African struggles for freedom in 1837 (the Sabinada revolt); 1839 (Manuel Balaio revolt), and 1847 (the Vassouras re-volt) must have clearly made Brazil difficult to rule for the busy em-peror Dom Pedro II (1831-1884). It is of interest to note that Dom Pedro II's daughter Princess Isabel abolished slavery (1888) while acting as regent in her father's absence. During this same period, "embranquecimento" became the official priority of Brazil.[26]

The African proverb, *"When the fool fails to darken ivory, he tries to whiten ebony,"* is informative here.[27] Note that for over 400 years Africans in Brazil knew they were African, knew that the Portuguese were the enemies of freedom, and continually fought and died in the service of freeing African people from slavery. The "embranquecimento" process has been in effect for about 115 years. While not complete, more than100 years of "embranquecimento" have done more psychic damage to the African than the 400 years of racist enslavement and colonial domination.

The power of "embranquecimento" is that it was a psychological assault on the Afro-Brazilian fundamental sense of what it means to be human. It was and is psychological terrorism at its most devious, demeaning, and devastating best. As Carter G. Woodson noted, "If you control a man's thoughts, you don't have to worry about his actions."[28] In an earlier discussion of Black psychology, it is noted, in similar regard, that "power is the ability to define reality and to have other people respond to your definition as if it were their own."[29] Clearly the most important reality to define is the meaning of one's own humanity. The "embranquecimento" process (memetic ideation) was an attempt by the Portuguese to re-define for Africans in Brazil what it means to be human. It, in effect, planted in the consciousness of both Black and white Brazilians the memetic ideas that goodness, success, creativity, genius, beauty, civilization, etc., were attributes of being Portuguese (white) and ultimately the idea that being human for Black people meant being white. In so doing they asserted that to be African was to be less than human and that through the process of "embranquecimento" (memetic ideation) the African could become human. Embranquecimento was and remains a systematic and sophisticated attempt to re-define for Africans in Brazil what it means to be human. Embranquecimento is psychological terrorism.

There was a time in the United States when older people would teach Black children that they had a kind of obligation or duty to "lighten up the race." Young people with dark complexions were not seen or judged to be as attractive or pretty as those with light complexions. Darker people were never seen as the "right choice" in a mate. Epithets of Black this or Black that, often proceeded by ugly, were common demeaning salutations directed at highly pigmented African Americans. The United States version of the Portuguese "embranquecimento" (whitening) or the Spanish "blanqueamiento" (whitening) was experienced as color consciousness (memetic ideation) and a debilitating shattered African consciousness and fractured Black identity.

Negation and nullification of Blackness permeates throughout society in the United States. For instance, the long struggle that Black artists waged to be included in the film industry was marked, and in many ways remains marked, by White standards of beauty (memetic ideations). From the Cotton Club of the 1920s to and through the "Blaxploitation films" of 1970s up to the Mega Black films of today, the marketability of Black stars was always determined by their acceptability to White taste and sensitivities (memetic ideations). Some Black sororities even instituted a "brown paper bag test" (memetic ideations) wherein one's complexion had to be lighter than a brown paper bag in order for one to be admitted into the sorority. In so doing, it was thought that the sorority would fulfill its duty to stay "bright and nearly white" (memetic ideation). In many cities and towns throughout the United States, little Black girls would demonstrate their physical agility and rhythmic acuity by playing double-dutch jump rope games. Often times their skill was matched against a rhyming chant that said, *"If you are white, you're all right; if you are brown, stick around and if you are Black, jump back (get out)"* (memetic ideation).[30] Reinforcing into the consciousness and identity of children the message that to be Black is to be by nature an inferior and deviant form of human being is tantamount to child abuse and neglect. Light skin and straight hair (memetic ideations) became, and in many ways still are, the undeniable badges of goodness and beauty. Lightness and closeness to whiteness (memetic ideations) become the standard of being human. It serves as the license for race-based privilege (memetic ideations) and the undeniable evidence of being worthy and good. Because it is a fundamental denial of one's own intrinsic human worth and value, the resultant desire for proximity to whiteness becomes a debilitating psychological condition that is pathological and destructive. "Embranquecimento," "blanquea-miento," color consciousness, "wanna be white," and self-hatred all result in a shattered African consciousness and fractured Black identity driven by a dysfunctional desire to be white.

Shattered African consciousness and fractured Black identity should be classified as pathogenic. Given this peculiar pathology for both continental and diasporan Africans, the on going and constant exposure to psychological terrorism in the form of imposed memetic ideations is an unidentified pathogen. Accordingly, those who have this uncontrollable and/or unexplainable desire to be white or who wish to have a proximity-to-whiteness, or have the illusion that they are not Black, should be clinically diagnosed as suffering from trauma.

The mental health of a people is an essential aspect of their human wellness and health. The consequence of White suprem-acy (racism) and its requisite negation and nullification of African people and things African (ideas, philosophy, history, and tradi-tions) have resulted in more everlasting damage than the whip or the physical chains of bondage. In fact, in a very real way, the physical damage and destruction of Black life was equal to, if not precipitated by, an insidious assault on the psychological value of African human beings. Next to anthropology, psychology and psychiatry have served as the fundamental disciplines and intel-lectual tools used to justify the dehumanization of African people. Psychology and psychiatry have been and remain critical instru-ments in the falsification and denigration of the image and mean-ing of African people. The mental assault on African people, which resulted in a worldwide perception and treatment of African people as inferior and less than human, was designed and conducted by White supremacists under the cloak of science. What, in fact, was created was an intellectual atmosphere that was intentionally designed to be destructive and detrimental to the mental health and well-being of all African people.

The Unfinished Revolution

Haiti's unfinished revolution must be understood in the context of African consciousness and its distortion. The African is distinguished by a particular consciousness that is reflected in a special capacity for having intelligence of the mind and heart. Every knowable and perceivable object in the natural universe is a hieroglyph of Divine consciousness (i.e., comprehension and imagination). In the sense of the Divine, African consciousness is, however, more than thinking, feeling, and awareness. Everything vibrates in a divinely governed universe. It is "potentiality" contained in itself and the entire universe as a never-ending totality of possibilities. This sense of African consciousness requires one to meet the challenges of awareness, knowing, comprehension, and existence through the realms of knowing and levels of awareness that are the very same aspects of being that one is attempting to define. African consciousness is, in effect, the intelligent energy of the Divine.

It is the hermeneutics of consciousness that determine how African people conceive of and understand themselves as fundamentally spirit. The awareness of oneself as spirit, in turn, allows one to access realms of knowing that are not limited to just cognition or perception. It also allows one to be accessible to and to access those spirits in the realm of the spirit. It connects knowing and awareness to both the perceivable (visible) and the unperceivable (invisible). Hence, consciousness is not bound by time, space, or place. It connects knowing, awareness, and comprehension to the universal and the Divine. Consciousness is that which gives congruity among the various realms of being.

The African sense of consciousness is thus both the substance (essence) and state (condition/effect) of all that exists and does not exist. It is the capacity to absorb all light (energy) and information. It is more than being simply aware. It is being aware, unaware, and beyond awareness at the same time. The African sense of consciousness is the essence, energy, expression, and experience of African people as the material (physical) and mental (non-physical) reflection of spirit and the vibratory evidence and energy of the Divine All. It is that which transcends thought and penetrates (absorbs) everything so as to make being African aware of itself.

It is consciousness that allows for the retention of ancestral sensibilities that interpret contemporary experience. Consciousness, in this case, functions as both retentive and residual knowledge and awareness. As retentive energy, it allows for the "remembering" or retention of all previous information, experience, and ideas. As residual energy, consciousness provides a conduit or circuit for tapping into the residue of human knowing and awareness and thereby creates or inspires new knowledge and awareness. Consciousness finally allows one to be aware of the possibility of one's (destiny's) fulfillment. It is Haitian consciousness, as awareness, knowing, and comprehension, and its subsequent meaning that gives particular content, context, and contour to Haitian character and style. Without an understanding of the vibratory energy that configured itself into being, becoming and belonging to African people, one is incapable of fully comprehending why Mackandal, Boukman, Toussaint, Dessalines, and other Black leaders reacted to and determined reality in a unique and special way.

The question of liberty and freedom and the ensuing Haitian struggle reads differently when discussed in the context of consciousness and the Haitian memetic complex. The convolution of the Haitian revolution becomes far more complex when the African consciousness of the people in struggle is explored as the consequence and cause of the movements and moments representing the revolution. One has to be careful not to explain consciousness erroneously. As stated above, the African sense of consciousness is both the essence and the state of the mind. Consequently, the idea of a "fractured consciousness" allows us to see the complexity of the cache comprised of opposing, complementary, conflicting, similar, and fundamentally different ideas. It requires a critical, detailed excavation of the mind maps of the actors.

Haitian society, in both its historical and contemporary unfolding, can best be understood through the pulse of Haitian consciousness as typified by the iconic leaders of the revolution. Haiti's contemporary social structure of elite Whites, privileged Mulattos, and poor Blacks could be viewed as the legacy of Haiti's historical cache of consciousness embedded in the mindset or mental map of Haiti's birth. The lives and thoughts of Francois Mackandal, Dutty Boukman, Cecile Fatiman, Toussaint L'Ouverture, Henry Christophe, and Alexandre Petion can be framed as a template of Haiti's contemporary cache of consciousness and a framework for revisiting its unfinished revolution.

While being the most African country in the Western hemisphere, from its inception, Haiti was marked with the presence of classism and White privilege. The turbulent years of Spanish, French, and American rule and domination can be seen as an ongoing terrorist assault on the African mind of Haitians caused by European and American thought and political interests. Ultimately, the endurance of France and Francophone beliefs and ideas became the hegemonic umbrella of Haitian life while Voodoo served as its grounding. Driven by the Code Noir, hegemonic Frenchness served to place whiteness and elitism as the cornerstone of Haitian life.

In a kind of perverted way, France's Ancien Regime of three estates translated or gave birth to a societal legacy of Haiti's tripartite social system of White elites, privileged so-called Mulattos, and poor Blacks. The memetic ideation that supported the Age of Enlightenment, and its bastard child the Age of Slaveocracy, infected Haiti's birth as an independent nation with ideas like aristocracy, class privilege, elitism, subjugation, apostolic authority, and the sanctity of whiteness in the form of being French. Through such a birth, not only is Whiteness privileged, the desire to be close to "Frenchness" was transfigured to being Haitian and/or honoring Haitian customs and behavioral norms that approximated being French.

Time and time again, throughout Haiti's history, African consciousness emerges as moments of meaning. Pregnant with the idea of being free and African, the life of Francois Mackandal represents such a moment. Given the lack of records and the filtering of Mackandal's moments, it is very difficult to illuminate Mackandal's consciousness with his own words. Nevertheless, one can extrapolate the contours and content of his story as a reflection of philosophy and worldview of the African population held in captivity in Saint Domingue during the 18th century. The worldview and beliefs of the Africans from West Central Africa (BaNtu-Kongo) and Guinea Coast (Aja, Fon, and Ewe) would have been the prevalent, especially the Bakongo, mindset in the enslaved community. These beliefs and ideas would have served as fertile soil for Mackandal's thinking and belief system. The common worldview of the Africans held captive in Saint Domingue would have supported the spiritual or sacred power of the "Bokor"[31] and the special "invisible" powers embedded in the natural world of flora and fauna. As a Maroon leader, he would have had to demonstrate his "powers;" and there is evidence that both members of the master class and the enslaved held Mackandal in high regard as a powerful healer. Hence, it would not have been difficult for him to attract and organize his fellow Africans.

As another indicator of his alignment with the beliefs of the African community, it is recorded that at one gathering, the community of enslaved Africans prostrated before Mackandal, a gesture that the African worldview would understand as indicative of high regard and deep respect for him and his position. His alignment with the beliefs of his people would have facilitated this gathering and the organization of the maroon and enslaved communities into a unified army of liberation. While Mackandal's struggle was interrupted by torture and betrayal, his moment should be seen as African liberation becoming pregnant.

Liberty's birth in Haiti was clearly midwifed by Dutty Boukman and Cecile Fatiman. As noted in Chapter Four, Cecile Fatiman's Lwa was Erzuli Danta, who belonged to the Petro families of "nanchons" (nations). The Petro Loa are generally fiery, hot, aggressive, and warlike. Erzuli Danta is often depicted as a scarred (indication of her country markings) and buxom Black woman holding a child protectively in her arms. She is a particularly fierce protector of women and children. Dutty Boukman was, in my opinion, a Bokar. He was the spirit of the guardian of life and the master of the invisible realm. At the Alligator Swamp, he admonishes Africa to "throw away the symbol of the god of the whites... and listen to the voice of liberty." The memetic ideation found in Boukman's consciousness was a "fearlessness" that aligned his mind map with a powerful and divinely governed universe and gave him an uncompromising belief in being free and African. Clearly, the Haitian revolution was midwifed by the spirits of the invisible realm that simultaneously called the enslaved to be African and to unleash a fiery hot energy that would protect life (i.e., women and children) and set them free.

The memetic ideations of Mackandal, Boukman, and Fatiman are found in the consciousness of those Haitians who aspire to be free and African, especially those who profess and honor Voodoo and those identified as the poor Blacks. As templars of African desire to be free and African, the cache of Mackandal, Boukman, and Fatiman's consciousness represents essential elements in the overall shattered consciousness and fractured identity of all Haitians.

Another aspect of Haitian shattered consciousness and fractured identity can be further explored in the life and thinking of Toussaint L'Ouverture. While having an African Arrada father, Toussaint's consciousness was infected at an early age with memetic ideas stemming from ideas found in Catholicism, Plutarch, Epicurus, and Raynal. Complicated by the retention of African memetic ideations, in the form of Vodun, Toussaint, nevertheless, paid special allegiance to France and the French ways of being. In his constitution of 1801, he specifically identified Saint Domingue as part of the French Empire and the Catholic, apostolic, Roman faith as the only publicly professed faith. Toussaint's mindset and consciousness was codified in the 1801 Haitian constitution, which stated that "there cannot exist slaves on this territory, servitude is therein forever abolished" and "all men are born, live and die free and French."[32] The cache of Toussaint's consciousness can be found in those Haitians who are phenotypically Black and have a strong identification with being Haitian yet aspire to acquire the affectations of being French. They secretly desire to be French and if able will vacation in France and send their children to France to be properly or better educated.

Jean-Jacques Dessalines represents another aspect of Haiti's shattered consciousness and fractured identity, which can serve as a template for one strata of the Haitian social system. Dessalines was born in Africa and imprinted with African ideas and beliefs, most likely in accord with a Guinean worldview. His capture resulted in his being sold to the French where he matured under the conditions of a torturous French plantation in the Northern Provence. Being tormented and brutalized by the French for over thirty years, he and his brothers were ultimately sold to a free Black named Dessalines. It is no small footnote that Jacque adopted the name Dessalines from his free Black owner and not the name Dukas from his French master. One has to ask what ideas, thoughts, and beliefs served as the substance of his consciousness. He learned from his contemporaries like L'Ouverture and Marie Jeanne La Martiniere. He liberated his wife from her French sexual exploiter, who used her as his mistress and sex slave. What memetic ideations did Dessalines internalize from the experience of French oppression and African ownership? In both instances he was held as a slave. Yet, he emerged in the revolution as essentially a Black nationalist. The memetic ideation constituting Dessalines' consciousness and mindset were thoughts and beliefs reflecting that Blacks and so-called mulattos had a common enemy, the French; the impetus for all things was a love of Black people, and white admiration was tempered with the recognition that while perceived as powerful, the whites should not be perceived as invincible.

Like L'Ouverture, Dessalines' mindset is, in fact, revealed through the language and ideas he authored and crafted as his 1805 Constitution. Shortly after winning independence from France, Haiti's revolutionary elite declared Jean-Jacque Dessalines as emperor. They so noted specifically,

We, H. Christophe, Clerveaux, Vernet, Gabart, Petion, Geffard, Toussaint, Brave, Raphael, Roamin, Lalondridie, Capoix, Magny, Daut, Conge, Magloire, Ambrose, Yayou, Jean Louis Franchois, Gerin, Mereau, Fervu, Bavelais, Martial Besse...As well in our name as in that of the people of Hayti... Do declare that the tenor of the present constitution is the free spontaneous and invariable expression of our hearts, and the general will of our constituents, and we submit it to the sanction of H.M. the Emperor Jacques Dessalines our deliverer, to receive its speedy and entire execution.[33]

Dessalines' constitution declared that "the people of Haiti have formed themselves into a free state, sovereign and independent of any other power in the universe."[34] The constitution went on to declare that "slavery is forever abolished; the citizens of Hayti are brothers; and equality in the eyes of the law is incontestably acknowledged."[35] Specifically, it also stated that "there cannot exist any titles, advantages, or privileges; the law will be applied to all; and that no person is worthy of being a Haitian who is not a good father, good son, a good husband, and especially a good soldier".[36] It is also interesting to note that as possibly a direct corrective to the inhumane practices of the French, Dessalines' constitution explicitly stated that "fathers and mothers are not permitted to disinherit their children; no white man of whatever nation he may be shall put his foot on this territory with the title of master or proprietor; and all Haytians shall hence forward be known only by the generic appellation of Blacks."[37] In effect, to be Haitian was to be free, responsible, and Black.

The cache of Dessalines' consciousness can be found in those Haitians who are phenotypically Black and have a strong identification with being Haitian with a yet-to-be tested admiration for things French in the guise of being Haitian. They love Haiti and hold onto the idea that the Blacks and so-called Mulattos are both Haitian, but just separated by money. They also believe that while the whites should not be perceived as invincible, their privilege should not be challenged.

Henri Christophe represents another aspect of Haiti's shattered consciousness and fractured identity, which can serve as a template for Haitian consciousness and as a template for one strata of the Haitian social system. Christophe represents an intriguing morphing of Haitian identity and consciousness. After the assassination of Dessalines, he made the northern state a "kingdom" and had himself ordained as Henri, King of Haiti, Sovereign of Tortuga, Gonave, and other adjacent islands; Destroyer of Tyranny, Regenerator and Benefactor of the Haitian nation, Creator of her moral, political, and martial institutions, First crown and Monarch of the New World, Defender of the faith, Founder of the Royal Military Order of Saint Henry. He renamed Cap Francais, so it became Cap Henri. He established royalty in Haiti and named his son Jacques-Victor heir apparent with the title Prince Royal of Haiti.

It should be recognized that Christophe has the recognition of being parented with ideas coming from his father, who was a freeman, and his mother, who was an enslaved African. The memetic ideation embedded in his mental map shaped by exposure to the White world included aristocracy, class privilege and position, racial categories, elitism, economic exploitation, theocracy, patriarchal domination, caste (permanent attribution), individualism, classism, and colorism. His mental map included ideations of regency, security, the savagery and treachery of the French, the importance of art and culture (European), and death before disgrace.

Ruling Haiti as King, Sovereign of Tortuga, Gonave, and other adjacent islands, Destroyer of Tyranny, Regenerator and Benefactor of the Haitian nation for almost a decade, Henri Jacques Christophe suffered a stroke in October 1820 that left him partially paralyzed. In this condition, Christophe ordered his attendants to bathe him and dress him in his formal military uniform, place him in his favorite chair in his den, and leave him alone. Shortly after the attendants left his side, Christophe committed suicide by shooting himself in the heart with a silver bullet; ergo, death before disgrace.

The cache of Christophe's consciousness can be found in those Haitians who are phenotypically Black and have a strong identification with being Haitian with a yet-to-be tested admiration for things French in the guise of being Haitian with a masked sense of aristocracy. They love Haiti and hold onto the idea that the Blacks and so-called Mulattos are both Haitian.

Alexandre Petion's cache of consciousness represents another aspect of Haiti's shattered consciousness and fractured identity, which can serve as a template for another strata or strand of the Haitian social system. The son of a wealthy White father and a free born "gens de coleur" mother, Alexandre was sent to France to be educated at the military academy in Paris. The Gens de Coleur represented a third class in the Haitian morphed retention of the French third estate. Petion's lived experiences included direct French acculturation, military indoctrination, witness to creole treachery, an unforgiving war between Blacks and so-called Mulattos, and the establishment of Haiti as a refuge and supporter of free and enslaved Africans' fight for freedom in South America. Petion represents the antecedent consciousness and mindset of the complicated privileged so-called mulatto. During the formation of the Haitian nation state, and continuing to this day, African unity on the island was and has been eroded by a Haitian conscious-ness that supports continued tensions that pit Blacks and so-called Mulattos against each other.

The complex mindset of Petion can be found in those Haitians who consciously and most often unconsciously see themselves as privileged, and undeniably Haitian with all of its African undertones. Yet they refuse to see and relinquish their role as a political and social buffer between the White elite and poor Blacks.

It is my contention that slavery, colonialism, and racial oppression created a meaning of Blackness that was contemptuous, denigrating, and nullifying. However, because the mind of the African also possessed African memetic ideations, racial oppression did not simply result in what W.E.B. Dubois' called a "double consciousness" or free flowing acculturation into French ideologies. However, one must look more deeply. In his now classic discussion of Negro identity, W.E.B. Dubois' insights are, in part, helpful in this context. Dubois notes that

After the Egyptian and Indian, the Greek and Roman, the Teuton and Mongolian, the Negro is a sort of seventh son born with a veil and gifted with second sight in this American world—a world which yields him no true self-consciousness, but only lets him see himself through the revelation of the other world. It is a peculiar sensation, this double consciousness, this sense of always looking at oneself through the eyes of others, of measuring one's soul by the tape of a world that looks on in amused contempt and pity. One ever feels his twoness —an American, a Negro; two souls, two thoughts, two unreconciled strivings; two warring ideals in one dark body, whose dogged strength alone keeps it from being torn asunder.[38]

In African American folklore, the seventh son is believed to have healing powers and be able to see the future. Where in the memetic consciousness of Dubois' African is found the capacity to heal and the ability to see the future? Dubois' double consciousness is more complex than just two warring identities. Dubois states that the Negro was "born with a veil," connoting having supernatural abilities and the gift of second-sight in a world which "yields him no sense of self-consciousness." Dubois says, "It is this peculiar sensation, this double consciousness, this condition of always looking at one's self through the eyes of others, of measuring one's soul by the tape of a world that looks in amused contempt and pity, which creates this double consciousness." Seen as memetic ideations, Dubois' double consciousness is revealing. Racial oppression as a memetic ideation, for instance, would result in the African, now as Haitian, to only see Blackness as an inferior color (being), through the revelation of the other (a French-white) world. Through the conflict of culture and consciousness, the African was made to see himself not as an African but as less than human or a Negro or nigger. The intention was not to produce a Black/White man (double consciousness) but a human who believed oneself to be less than human. The fundamental question here is who or what is sensing? Is it the Black sensing the white or the White sensing the Black or is it some other element? Because

Dubois was not using an African episteme and had little opportunity to reflect on African understandings of reality, his otherwise insightful genius was inaccurate in this matter.

Dubois' error and our further understanding of the Haitian cache of consciousness can be clarified or corrected with the use of African concepts to understand African reality. Herein the BaKongo idea of *"Kizungu Zongu"* (Tornadoes of the Mind) to represent African shattered consciousness and fractured identity is helpful.

Kizungu Zongu (Spirit Defilement) and Haiti's Cache of Consciousness

"Kizungu Zongu," as tornadoes of the Mind, should be thought of as a kind of spirit defilement or damage for African people. It is defilement in the sense of being disconnected from one's spirit (even though one is highly spiritual) and having a sense of not being truly or completely human by internalizing an unchallenged belief in one's human inferiority. It is the profound sense that in being disconnected or spirit damaged that one's being is representative of human nullification and negation. In many ways, psychologically, diasporan Africans in the U.S., Cuba, Haiti, and Brazil suffer from Kizungu Zongu, Tornadoes of the Mind, which expresses itself as "spirit illness" not mental illness.

Clearly slavery's aftermath persists in the forms of racism, cultural domination, and identity confusion throughout the world. It was and is an important determinant in the psychological development of African people in North America, Central America, South America, and the West Indies and Africa. If, and only when, the African meanings of being human are removed from the center (ergo, Afrocentricity) of African people's consciousness can African people be permanently enslaved.

The process of shattering African consciousness and fracturing Black identity is the key lingering effect of the enslavement process. This examination of Haiti as an island of "memes" resulting in "Kizungu Zongu," "Tornadoes of the Mind," helps to ultimately recognize the world-wide historical and contemporary processes that were designed to destroy and/or disrupt the human meaning of being African.

It was (is), in fact, a worldwide phenomenon integrally bound to the process of "westernization." In this regard, the experience of Africans everywhere in the Diaspora was formulaic. The mass kidnapping, sale, and enslavement of Africans from the 16th through the 19th centuries was one of the most devastating criminal enterprises in recorded human history. Colonization and chattel slavery brought genocide to African identity, history, culture, and consciousness and seriously damaged Africans' ability to imagine, manage, and maintain African-based systems of human development and governance. It created "Kizungu Zongu." Replacing the "spiritness" of the African with a set of new loyalties was achieved by making the meaning of being African correspond to being human only to the extent that it approximates White definitions of humanity. Chattel slavery and colonization caused Africa's natural developmental trajectory to be derailed, resulting in African people's, as well as others', failure to see African thought, values, and beliefs as being essential to addressing the critical questions of life and living. Seldom are African ideas seen as having full and equal value in the understanding, planning, and determination of the future of human affairs.

The process of "chattelization" and colonization, as psychological warfare, enriched the perpetrators of slavery at the expense of the victims of enslavement in the Americas and of colonization in Africa. The legacy of "chattelization" and colonization continues to enrich the descendants of the perpetrators while maintaining, through continual westernization, the underdevelopment of Africa and impoverishing Africans and descendants of Africans in the Diaspora.

Ultimately the lingering psychological effects of the Trans-Trans-Atlantic Slave Trade experience can be simply seen as the shattering of African consciousness and the fracturing of Black identity. However, both of these effects are symptomatic of a deeper assault on the African, which is more significant than mental illness.

While in some ways it is easier to identify the pathologies found in people victimized by racism, White supremacy, and oppression, it is somewhat more difficult to articulate a people's normal or natural functioning in the absence of their victimization. Having been under psychological siege for so long, many African people have come to believe that their reactions and accommodations to oppression and victimization are, in fact, their normal or natural way of being.

One can imagine that many Haitians as well as many Africans on the continent and throughout the rest of the diaspora have accepted the idea of the unworthiness of being African for so long (several generations) or have substituted the false identity of being an "individual" that they no longer perceive the assault on their human worth and well-being. Almost like being in a state of extreme shock where the body no longer senses the pain, many Africans no longer sense the value or importance of being African. They are simply "individuals." They are in an historical state of psychological trauma resulting from mentacide.[39] In such a state of "Kizungu Zongu," they take refuge in declaring and defending the state of being not African or in finding their primary identity in "place" (i.e., Haiti, Jamaica, Brazil, American, urban, northern, etc.).

Given the analysis provided in this review, it is believed that for African people, the most profound and lingering effect of enslavement and colonization has been "Kizungu Zongu" resulting from being infected with or assaulted by long-standing, ongoing sensorial informational structures (memetic infection) representing the chattelization and dehumanization of African people.

While "Kizungu Zongu" or "Tornadoes of the Mind" can be seen or experienced as self-alienation at the personal level, it is far more dangerous than simply feeling the sense of not being oneself. "Kizungu Zongu" for African people is the sense of be-ing disconnected from one's spirit (i.e., traumatized disconnected spirits (TDS)) and thereby having a sense of not being truly or completely human. It is the profound sense that by being disconnected or spiritless, one's being is representative of human nullification and negation. "Kizungu Zongu" contaminates the collective energy field such that almost every single African has a constant feeling of dis-at-ease, incompleteness, and a need for over-compensation. The consciousness and identity of African people is, at some degree, wrought with fear, anxiety, insecurity, anger, hostility, anomaly, and ignorance. In effect, rather than suffer from a "double consciousness," the simple notion of identification with the aggressor or the unjustifiable desire to acculturate or to dem-onstrate one's materialism through acquisition of goods means collectively that we suffer from "Kinzungu Zongu" as a lingering effect of enslavement and colonization,.

The fragile and tattered societal fabric of Haiti's social struc-ture, pillared by "White elitism," "Privileged Mulattism," and "poor Blackism," is an impermeable netting that should be seen as the "waste matter" of the cache of culture and consciousness in the soul of Haiti. The beliefs and behaviors of Haiti's White elite, privileged Mulattos, and poor Blacks are in many ways the simultaneous playing forward of Mackandal's African consciousness in captivity with Boukman's resistance to containment; Toussaint 's embrace of French superiority; Dessalines' instinctual rescue of the African mind; Christophe's sorrowful attempt at planting Euro-pean models in African soil; Petion's attempt at compromise and acculturation; and Papa Doc's eroding corruption of traditional African thought and practice.

Today, the White elite, privileged Mulatto, and the poor Black in Haiti will all forcefully declare themselves to be Haitian. Yet in this place called Haiti, under the banner of Haiti, you will find a social stratum of privilege and denigration as rigid as America's racial segregation, South Africa's apartheid, and India's caste system. For all Haitians, the rigid psychological boundaries that separate the White elite, privileged so-called Mulattos, and poor Blacks are as impermeable as they are invisible. It is this cache of consciousness with its complex holding of conflicting and competing memetic ideations that makes it so. The White elite consciousness while extolling to be Haitian (and pure) is infected with memetic ideations supporting beliefs in the superiority of things French.

The privileged Mulattos while equally extolling being Haitian (and mixed) are infected with memetic ideations that support the notion that some Haitians are "better" than other Haitians. In this same mental place, there are poor Blacks who proudly claim to be Haitian and Black; and they own a consciousness infected with memetic ideations supportive of African beliefs and traditions whose very value is challenged as savage and primitive at every moment and turn.

Haiti's internal shattered consciousness and fractured identity and external anti-African memetic ideations combine to undermine Haiti's hard won freedoms during the twentieth century. "Kinzungu Zongu" (i.e., shattered consciousness and fractured identity) has allowed foreign governments and investors to exploit Haiti's fragile position to maximize non-Haitian profit and trade. It has equally allowed Haiti to fester in self-inflected wounds of internal psychic trauma. Consequently, the world sees an African nation-state in the Western hemisphere in self-denial. Due to its untreated "Kinzungu Zongu" (tornadoes of the mind), resulting from memetic infections, Haiti presents itself as a country plagued with political instability, mismanagement, corruption and oppression, collective suffering, and underdevelopment.

The contemporary and continuing legacy of Haiti's complex cache of consciousness must be addressed and healed if the aftermath of the destructive earthquake of 2010 is to be successfully resolved. Haiti's shattered African consciousness and fractured Black identity were the structural barrier to the success of Haiti's enslaved Africans' desire to be fully free and African. And today, the residuals and retentions of that very same shattered African consciousness and fractured Black identity is the functional barrier to Haiti's rising up from the mental rubble of the 2010 earthquake.

The cache of consciousness represented by and reflected in the lives of Mackandal, Boukman, L'Ouverture, Dessalines, Christophe, Petion, and on up to Papa Doc represent the framing and distortion of Haitian consciousness and society. In fact, one could argue that the consciousness of these major architects of Haiti's quest for liberty can also serve as the iconic templates for understanding Haiti's unfinished revolution.

Haiti's unfinished revolution as well as the struggles of Africans throughout the diaspora and on the continent must openly, unashamedly, and unapologetically give recognition and respect to the grounding in African wisdom traditions and spirit science that privileges the idea of a "Pan African Humanism" as an expansion of Mphahlele's notion of African humanism.[40]

The concept of "Pan African Humanism" would require that an adequate psychological understanding of African consciousness and Black identity worldwide and would require engagement with all forms of African intellectual, religious, literary, and artistic production across time and space. Pan African Humanism would support the use of an African centered paradigm that privileges the life experiences, history, and traditions of people of African ancestry as guidelines for healing and restoration. Pan African Humanism asserts as an organizing precept the centrality of African cultural realities and experiences for African people and the principles of location and agency for viewing, understanding, and replicating African phenomena. Its adoption would represent the intellectual, philosophical, political, and spiritual foundations upon which people of African ancestry create their own scientific and moral criteria for authenticating the reality of African human processes.[41] As a paradigm for development, it would give license to an African centered way that represents the core and fundamental qualities of the *"being," "belonging," and "becoming"* of people of African ancestry. Accordingly, Haiti's unfinished revolution and those incomplete efforts on the continent and throughout the diaspora will only be successfully completed when African life is cherished, and the human spirit is well, whole, and healthy.

In finishing the revolution, Haiti's irritated genie should have created a universal mindset wherein being human and African is characterized by confidence, competence, and a consciousness of the sense of full possibility and unlimited potential. In achieving this, the Haitian revolution should have tapped into the most fundamental and essential core African root and spiritual source for inspiring health and eliminating imbalance and discord in order to re-establish and/or restore African harmony and optimal human functioning.

Inspired by the spark in the Dismal Swamp, today's African revolutionary spirit worldwide has to heal the shattered African consciousness and the fractured Black identity by being one African family. The African family can only become viable, healthy, and whole when African people help to shape modern society with rules and relationships that affirm African humanity. This can only be done when Africans approach our collective wellness, social, and political life by agreeing to rescue and honor our common being and belonging and by venerating our common ancestry. This can be achieved by researching and celebrating our common family genealogy, stories, and history across time and place.

In addition, the restoration of African wellness and optimal human functioning must enhance the cultural grounding of family dynamics and protocols. It must also advance the knowledge of eldership, parenting, and governance and provide opportunities for inter-familial and Pan African bonding and relationships. Equally important, African health and well-being must prioritize family-centered (as distinct from individualized) growth and development and create activities that foster unity, personal connection, and African family loyalty. The invention/re-invention of both traditional and contemporary African centered rituals and customs that foster bonding and kinship must be given priority. By engaging in cooperative sustenance activities, defending African family-centered conflict resolution and protecting the African family's authority, rights, and responsibilities, we can minimize internal conflict, crises, and disintegration of African life and living and maximize intergenerational transfer of wealth, wisdom, development, and socialization. Lastly, by revisiting the worldwide exchange of capital, resources, and commerce grounded in African thought and values, African people can better critique and correct capitalism and socialism as well as any other forms of marketplace economies based in Africa's best interest and image. In so doing, the unfinished revolution will be able to meet the challenges of the new millennium.

The restoration of African consciousness and the re-estab-lishment of a recognized, respected, and vital African humanity in Haiti, and everywhere Africa's children live, is the charge of Haiti's unfinished revolution. The worldwide African revolution is not yet finished, and our ancestors require that we finish the job.

---

[1]   This is an excerpt from Pat Roberts' broadcast of The 700 Club Television Ministry on January 13, 2010. The segment discussed the devastation, suffering and humanitarian effort that was needed in Haiti after the 7.0 magnitude earthquake. Dr. Robertson spoke about Haiti's history and the 1791 slave rebellion led by Boukman Dutty at Bois Caiman. He asserted that Haiti's revolutionary history grounded in Voodo, combined with the horrible state of the country in modern times, has led countless scholars and religious figures over the centuries to believe the country is cursed and heavily implied that the earthquake was God's wrath.

[2]   From Holloway, J. Ed. (1991, p. 11). *Africanisms in American Culture.*

[3]   From Fu-Kiau, K. (2001, pp. 17-43). *Tying the Spiritual Knot: African Cosmology of the Bantu-Kôngo Principles of Life and Living.*

[4]   From Peek, P. & Yankah, K. (2003, p. 89). *African folklore: An Encyclopedia.* See also Akyaw, K.O. (2000, pp. 11-18). *A Profile of Nana Abass.*

[5]   See Appendix 3, Haiti's 1805 Constitution, Preliminary Declaration, Article 14.

[6]   Fu-Kiau, K. (2001, p. 47). *Tying the Spiritual Knot: African Cosmology of the Bantu-Kôngo Principles of Life and Living.*

[7]   Fu-Kiau, Personal communication, 2013.

[8]   As a requirement for diplomatic recognition, in 1825 France demanded that the Republic of Haiti pay a FRF150 million indemnity (comparable to US$12.7 billion as of 2009) in claims over property lost (captive Africans, infrastructure materials, etc.) resulting from the Africans freeing themselves from bondage in the Haitian revolution. In 2003, President of Haiti Jean-Bertrand Aristide demanded that France pay Haiti over 21 billion U.S. dollars (equivalent in today's money of the 90 million gold francs) Haiti was forced to pay Paris after winning its freedom from France. Following the 2004 Haitian coup d'état that overthrew President Aristide, the interim government led by Prime Minister Gérard Latortue (brought back from the U.S.) rescinded the reparations demand, calling it "foolish" and "illegal."

[9] From McGarrity, G. & Cárdensa, O. (1995, p. 78). "Cuba" in *No longer invisible: Afro-Latin Americas Today*. Minority Rights Group (Ed.).

[10] From McGarrity, G. & Cárdensa, O. (1995, p. 88). "Cuba" in *No longer invisible: Afro-Latin Americas Today*. Minority Rights Group (Ed.). It should be noted that the 1868 revolution began as pro-slavery and evolved after 1871 to be in support of freeing the enslaved (pro-abolition).

[11] See McGarrity, G. & Cárdensa, O. (1995, p. 87).

[12] See McGarrity, G. & Cárdensa, O. (1995, p. 87).

[13] See McGarrity, G. & Cárdensa, O. (1995, pp. 77-108).

[14] From Muhammad, J. (1995, pp. 163-180). "Mexico and Central America: Mexico." in *No longer Invisible: Afro-Latin Americas Today*. Minority Rights Group (Ed.).

[15] See Muhammad, J. (1995, p.163).

[16] See Muhammad, J. (1995, p.163).

[17] See Muhammad, J. (1995, pp.163-180).

[18] See McGarrity, G. & Cárdensa, O. (1995, pp. 86-94).

[19] In discussing Mexico and Central America's African heritage by referencing an early 1946 study by an Afro-Mexican scholar named Gunzalo Aguirre Beltran who investigated and documented the African presence in the predominantly Black town of Cuajinicuilapa in the state of Guerrero in Mexico.

[20] From Nascimento, A. (1979, p. 65). *Brazil Mixture or Massacre? Essays in the Genocide of a Black People*.

[21] From Vieira, R. (1995, pp. 19-46). "Brazil," in *No longer invisible: Afro-Latin Americas Today*. Minority Rights Group (Ed.).

[22] Veira, R. (1995, p. 28).

[23] For a detailed discussion of African resistance to enslavement in Brazil, see Leal, G. (2001, 291-313). "Fárígá/Ìfaradà: Black Resistance and Achievement in Brazil" in *African Roots, American Culture: Africa in the Creation of the Americas*. S. Walker (Ed.). The reader should also review Nascimento, A., Nascimento, E. & Nascimento. A. (1992). *Africans in Brazil: A Pan-African Perspective*, as well as Soumonni, L. & Barry, B. (Eds.) (2008). *Africa, Brazil and the Construction of Trans-Atlantic Black Identities*.

[24] Leal, G. (2001, p. 291-300).

[25] Bahia was and remains the location of the largest African population in Brazil. The Sastre rebellion was an early attempt to establish a free and independent government, but the attempt was defeated, and all the leaders were hanged. See Vieira, R. (1995, p. 31), "Brazil" in *No Longer Invisible: Afro-Latin Americas Today*. Minority Rights Group (Ed.).

[26] Viera, R. (1995, pp.31-32).

[27] Viera, R. (1995, p. 28). This proverb has passed on from generation to generation without written sourcing.

[28] This famous quote from Carter G. Woodson's *The Miseducation of the Negro* (1933, p. 84) is a powerful example of mental oppression.

[29] In 1983 at the New Era, Conference of scholars and theologians on emerging religious theologies in Madeira, Portugal, I introduced the definition of power as "the ability to define reality and to have other people respond to your definition as if it were their own and that the most important reality to define is the meaning of one's own human beingness." My definition has been adopted by African centered scholars and many others in the social and behavioral sciences.

[30] This is a saying that has no identifiable author. It is part of the historical folklore and folk sayings of the African American community. Most African Americans 40 and older are familiar with this saying. Big Bill Broonzy, born in 1893, was a prolific blues singer, songwriter, and guitarist, and in the 1920s, he reportedly sang about America's *Jim Crow* system, using the lyrics, *If you is white, you's alright, if you's brown, stick around, but if you's black, hmm, hmm, brother, get back, get back, get back*. See *I Feel so good: The life and times of Big Bill Broonzy* R. Riesman, 2011, Chicago: University of Chicago Press.

[31] It is important to note that the term or title of "Bokor" has been so demonized that most references to it identify it as a practitioner of "Black Magic" or evil. To the contrary, the Bokor, as discussed in chapter four (the Boko), is one who is knowledgeable in "Bo" and is highly respected by the people.

[32] See Appendix 2, Haiti's 1801 Constitution, Article 3.

[33] See Appendix 3, Haiti's 1805 Constitution.

[34] See Appendix 3, Haiti's 1805 Constitution, Preliminary Declaration, Article 1.

[35] See Appendix 3, Haiti's 1805 Constitution, Preliminary Declaration, Article 3.

[36] See Appendix 3, Haiti's 1805 Constitution, Preliminary Declaration, Article 9.

[37] See Appendix 3, Haiti's 1805 Constitution, Preliminary Declaration, Article 14.

[38] See, *The souls of black folks*, W. Dubois, 1903, NY: Dover Publications, Inc., first published by A.C. McClung and Co. Chicago.

[39] Dr. Bobby Wright introduced the concept of "Mentacide" as an important diagnostic in Black Psychology. "Mentacide" Dr. Wright defined as the "deliberate and systematic destruction of a group's minds with the ultimate objective being the extirpation of the group." "Mentacide," he believed to be a worldwide phenomenon being implemented against the entire Black race.

[40] See, "Images of the African personality," Mphahlele, E. (1987). Paper presented at Conference on Black Culture and Business. Johannesburg.

[41] Both Dr. Molefi Asante (2003) and Dr. Maulana Karenga (2010) have offered important definitions of Afrocentricity that support the unpacking of an African grand narrative.

Afterword

There is, in fact, no word after for Dr. Nobles' monumental discourse *The Island of Memes: Haiti's Unfinished Revolution.* It truly is an invitation to begin and not end an important and radically new conversation among African intellectuals and activists alike.

The application of Black psychology and African centered thought to the re-analyses of the Haitian revolution give us, in my opinion, the missing link in understanding our reaction and response to chattel enslavement and colonialism. Black psychology allows us to see the effects of enslavement and colonialism on the mind, consciousness, and identity of African peoples. The further evolution of Black psychology as a discipline using the methodology of Sakhu Djaer expands our ability to see for the first time the depth of African character, culture, and consciousness. Sakhu Djaer is our doorway to a more accurate understanding of our political, economic, cultural, and social realities.

In this text, Dr. Nobles has introduced us not just to a new paradigm for investigating the human experience, but he has expanded the boundaries of acceptable inquiry and broadened the concept of what is possible by his introduction of the concept of Sakhu Sheti/Djaer. As he defines it, Sakhu Sheti/Djaer is the process of understanding, examining, and explicating the meaning, nature, and functioning of being human for African people by conducting a deep, profound and penetrating search, study, and mastery of the process of "illuminating" the human spirit or essence and experience while engaging in the exploration of every aspect of reality, including the unseen. This is the missing strategy for truly understanding who we are, what happened to us, and where we must go in order to be well and whole.

In this manuscript, as a Black psychologist or more accurately a Sakhu Djaerist, Dr. Nobles uses Haiti as a case study of African liberation and sovereignty to address the question of African Consciousness and Black Identity in a way that penetrates the mental blockage impeding our understanding of the whole African experience. In utilizing the concept of "meme" and "memetic infection," he skillfully provides us with a deeper view into the historical experience of African peoples. While focusing on Haiti and the architects of African liberation, he has provided us with a new African centered historiography and analytical template that doesn't just describe and explain "what was done to us in history" but "why" we did or did not create successful and everlasting historical movements and moments. His introduction of "memes" and "memetic infection" as a theoretical template for understanding the derailment of African historical consciousness and identity requires careful and deliberate study. His identification of "sensoria-information structures" in the form of symbols, images, feelings, words, ideas, customs, practices, or any knowable and perceptible item or substance as any contagious information pattern that by symbiotically infecting human minds and altering behavior to reinforce the memetic idea is critical to our understanding of colonialism (neo- and first order), acculturation, and the difficulty of African nation-building and self-rule.

In *The Island of Memes: Haiti's Unfinished Revolution,* Dr. Nobles asserts that the contagious information pattern that replicated itself in Haiti, via infecting the minds of the enslaved Africans, was an identifiable complex of ideas and experiences that supported the belief that the African was "chattel" and void of human value and worth. The African memetic ideation offered a counter ideological position of being "free and African." Dr. Nobles is convincing in showing the damage done to the African mind, consciousness, and identity. He is equally convincing in showing the African as an expression of what is called Divine essence. In his discourse, Dr. Nobles painstakingly describes the African consciousness as preserving itself as a part of every and all things, yes, as the totality of creating, and expressing itself as individual and collective interdependence and yet one. He shows the individual as conscious of one's individuality while conscious of the fact that one is but an expression of the totality of the whole (the collective).

In his discourse on Haiti, Dr. Nobles has given us the tools needed to examine the total African experience before, during, and after enslavement and colonialism. He describes "the disconnected spirit," the phenomena of shattered African consciousness and fractured Black identity. He informs us that this syndrome of a traumatized disconnected spirit in the human family, a shattered African consciousness, and fractured Black identity is a result of contact with and domination by white people and their worldview which requires the dehumanization and de-Africanization of the African. In this context, Dr. Nobles states that retention of African Memetic Ideation is a key to understanding Haitian and all diaspora African consciousness.

In digesting Dr. Nobles' words, the reader, I believe, gets a much clearer picture of the results of the clashing of African and European culture and civilization. With the tool of Sakhu Sheti, you will be able to grasp the essential psychological aspect of African spirituality in the formation of diasporan African consciousness. You will also better understand the culture and consciousness that informed African (both continental and diasporan) behavior, beliefs, and actions from one generation to the next.

As an afterword leading to a new way forward, I would like to point out the international relevance of this work. Recently in an address at the 10th anniversary celebration of Pan-African Parliament in Johannesburg, South Africa (March 18, 2014), H. E. Jerry John Rawlings, former President of the Republic of Ghana, called on Africans to stop being passive observers as the developed world interferes and intervenes in the affairs of the continent. In calling upon the unification of Africa, he further noted that Africans cannot look on while elected presidents are plucked out of their countries everywhere in the African world and humiliated, disrespected, and disregarded. He charged that we, Africans, are equally to blame for looking on as the global powers enter our continent and virtually stage coups in our countries. This African inability and disunity, as referenced by President Rawlings and documented by Dr. Nobles, is a direct result of a shattered African consciousness and fractured Black Identity resulting from memetic infection.

In presenting this book to the world, Dr. Nobles has performed an invaluable intellectual service. It is a must read for anyone, especially the African Union, the Congressional Black Caucus, intellectuals, political activists, and nation builders worldwide who want to understand the state of not just the consciousness of African peoples but of all people who have suffered slavery, colonialism, and the false notion of white supremacy.

As noted, there is no afterword to *The Island of Memes: Haiti's Unfinished Revolution.* It is simply and profoundly a call for the basis of a new conversation for liberation.

— Prof. James Small (El Hajji Amin Ash Shaheed)
Baba L'orisa of Oya Kenney Cyrus Ila Ajuba of Trinidad/Tobago, The West Indies

Bibliography

Akbar, N. (1984). Africentric social science for human liberation. *Journal of Black Studies,* 14(4), 395-414.

Akbar, N. (1990). African American consciousness and Kemet: Spirituality, symbolism and duality in reconstructing kemetic culture. In M. Karenga (Ed.), *Papers, perspectives, projects,* 99-114. Los Angeles: University of Sankore Press.

Aristide, J. (2011). *Haiti-Haitii? phiolosophical reflections for mental decolonization,* Boulder, CO & London, UK: Paradigm Publishers.

Asante, M. (1980). *Afrocentricity* (revised). Trenton, NJ: Africa World Press.

Asante, M. & Mazama, A. (Eds.) (2008). *Encyclopedia of African religion.* Thousand Oaks, CA: Sage Publications.

Baptiste, S. & Relly, J.R. (1863). *Toussaint l'Ouverture: a biography and autobiography.* Chapel Hill, NC: University of North Carolina.

Barnhart, R. (2003). *Chambers dictionary of etymology.* Edinburgh, Scotland: Chambers Harrap Publishers Ltd.

Bell, C. (2004). *Revolution, romanticism, and the Afro-Creole protest tradition in Louisiana, 1718-1868.* Baton Rouge, LA: Louisiana State University Press.

Bellegarde, D. (2002). *Histoire du people (1492-1952) Port-au-Prince.* In D. Geggus (Ed.), *Haitian Revolutionary Studies* (p. 80). Bloomington, IN: Indiana University Press.

Blier, S. P. (1995). *African voodun: Art, Psychology and power.* Chicago: University of Chicago Press.

Bryan, P. (1984). *The haitian revolution and its effects.* London, UK: Heinemann Educational Publishers, Athenaeum Press Ltd.

Bulhan, H. (1985). *Frantz Fanon and the psychology of oppression.* New York: Plenum Press.

Carroll, W. (1997). *Isabel of Spain: The Catholic queen.* Front Royal, VA: Christendom Press.

Carruthers, J. (1985). *The irritated genie: An essay on the Haitian revolution.* Chicago: The Kemetic Institute.

Chamberlain, M. (1999). *The scramble for Africa* (2nd ed.). London: Longman.

Cheesman, C. (2007). *The armorial of Haiti: Symbols of nobility in the reign of Henry Christophe.* London: The College of Arms.

Child, L. and Karcher, C.L. (1833) *Appeal in favor of that class of Americans called Africans.* Amherst: University of Massachusetts Press.

Clive, C. (2007). *The Armorial of Haiti: Symbols of Nobility in the Reign of Henry Christophe.* London: The College of Arms.

Crowe, S. (1981). *The Berlin West African* conference, 1884-1885 (New ed.). New York: Longmans.

Corbett, B. *The Haitian revolution of 1791-1803, an historical essay in four parts.* Retrieved from http://www.webster.edu/~corbetre/haiti/history/revolution/revolution1.htm.

Danticat, E. (2005). *Anacaona: golden flower, Haiti 1490.* New York: Scholastic Inc.

Davidson, M. (1997). *Columbus then and now: a life re-examined.* Norman, OK: University of Oklahoma Press.

Davis, M. (1997). *Francois Macandal: The true story, facts, myths and legends.* Retrieved from http://www.macandal.org/paper.html.

Dawkins, R. (2010). *The Greatest show on earth: the evidence for evolution.* New York: Free Press.

Deren, M. (1953). *Divine horsemen: The living gods of Haiti.* Kingston, NY: McPherson & Company.

Dubois, L. (2004). *Avengers of the new world: The story of the Haitian revolution.* Cambridge, MA: First Harvard University Press.

DuBois, W.E.B. (1903). *The souls of black folks.* NY: Dover Publications, Inc., Chicago: A.C. McClung and Co.

Durkheim, E. & Halls, W. D. (1984). *The division of labor in society.* New York: Free Press.

Emmer, P. (1998). *The Dutch in the Atlantic economy, 1580-1880:* Trade, slavery and emancipation. In *Variorum Collected Studies Series* CS614.

Fanon, F. (1967). *Black skins, white masks.* New York: Grove Press, Inc.

Fick, C. (1990). *The making of Haiti: The Saint Domingue revolution from below.* Knoxville, TN: University of Tennessee.

Filan, K. (2007). *The Haitian Vodou Handbook.* Rochester, Vermont: Destiny Books.

Förster, S., Mommsen, W. & Robinson, R. (1989). *Bismarck, Europe, and Africa: The Berlin Africa conference 1884-1885 and the onset of partition.* Oxford, UK: Oxford University Press.

Fu-Kiau, K. (2001). *Tying the spiritual knot: African cosmology of the Bantu-Kongo.* (2nd ed.). Canada: Athelia Henrietta Press.

Gaines, A. D. (Ed.). (1992). *Ethnopsychiatry: The cultural construction of professional and folk psychiatries.* Albany, NY: State University of New York Press.

Geggus, D. (2002). *Haitian revolutionary studies.* Bloomington, IN: Indiana University Press.

Girard, P. R. (2011). *The slaves who defeated Napoleon, Toussaint L'Ouverture and the Haitian war of independence, 1801-1804.* Tuscaloosa: University of Alabama Press.

Goetz, Kathy, (Ed.). African American Families: It Takes a Whole Village To Raise a Child. *Family Resource Coalition Report;* v12 nl (29p) Spr 1993. Chicago.

González, A., Jackson, G., Pellicer, J. & Vinson, B. (2011). *Afro-Mexico: Dancing between myth and reality.* Austin, TX: University of Texas Press.

Goodell, W. (1853). *The American slave code in theory and practice: Its distinctive features shown by its statutes, judicial decisions, and illustrative facts.* New York, American and Foreign Anti-Slavery Society.

Griffin, N. (1992). *A short account of the destruction of the Indies.* Retrieved from: en.wikipedia.org/wiki/A_Short_Account_of_the_Destruction_of_the_Indies.

Griggs, E. & Prator, C. (Eds). (1968). *Henry Christophe and Thomas Clarkson: A correspondence.* Retrieved from: http://www2.webster.edu/~corbetre/haiti/history/revolution/revolution1.htm.

Grills, C. & Rowe, D. (1998). African traditional medicine: Implications for African-centered approaches to healing. In R. Jones (Ed.). *African American mental health* (pp. 71-102). Hampton, VA: Cobb & Henry.

Haq, M. and Sen, A. (1990). *The human development concept.* United Nations Development Program, the Creative Commons Attribution 3.0 IGO license at https://creativecommons.org/.

Hegel, G. (1966). *The phenomenology of the mind.* London: Allen and Unwin.

Helg, A. (1995). *Our rightful share: The Afro-Cuban struggle for equality, 1886-1912.* Raleigh, NC: University of North Carolina Press.

Higgins, C. (1994). *Feeling the spirit: Searching the world for the people of Africa.* New York: Bantam Books.

Hilliard III, A. (1986). The wisdom of kemetic governance. In M. Karenga & J. Carruthers (Eds.). *Kemet and the African worldview.* Los Angeles: University of Sankore Press.

Holloway, J. (Ed.) (1991). *Africanisms in American culture.* Bloomington, IN: Indiana University Press.

The Holy Bible (1973). International Version, International Bible Society.

Hood, R. (1994). *Begrimed and Black: Christian traditions on Blacks and blackness.* Minneapolis: Fortress Press.

Hochschild, A. (1999). *King Leopold's ghost: A story of greed, terror, and heroism in colonial Africa.* Boston: Houghton Mifflin Co.

James, C. (1989). The Black Jacobins. Vantage Books Ed. New York: Random House, Inc.

Jones-Gwynn, P. *The Amorial of Haiti: symbols of nobility in the reign of Henry Christophe.* Retrieved from http://www.college-of-arms.gov.uk/Haiti.pdf.

Jones, R. (Ed.). (1972). *Black psychology.* New York: Harper & Row.

Kambon, K. (1992). *The African personality in America: An African centered framework.* Tallahassee, FL: Nubian Nation Publications.

Karenga, M. (1988). Black studies and the problematic of a paradigm: The philosophical dimension, *Journal of Black Studies,* 18(4), 395-414.

Kelly, G. (1972). Notes on Hegel's "Lordship and Bondage." In A. MacIntyre (Ed.) *A Collection of critical essays* (pp. 189-217). Notre Dame, IN: University of Notre Dame Press.

King, L., Dixon, V. & Nobles, W. (Eds.). (1976). *African philosophy: Assumptions and paradigms for research on black persons.* J. Alfred Cannon Research Conference Series. Los Angeles: Fanon Research & Development Center.

Kojeve, A. (1969). *Introduction to the reading of Hegel.* New York: Basic Books.

Langton, Christopher G. (1995) *Artificial life an overview.* Boston: MIT Press.

Leal, G. (2001). Fariga/ifarada: Brazil resistance and achievement in Brazil. In S. Walker. (Ed.). *African roots, American culture: Africa in the creation of the Americas.* New York: Rowman & Littlefield Publishers, Inc.

Liss, P. K. (1992). *Isabel the Queen: life and times.* London: Oxford University Press.

L'Ouverture, T. (1863). *Toussaint L'Ouverture: A biography and autobiography.* Retrieved from http://books.google.com/books/about/Toussaint_L_Ouverture.html?id=BPYCAAAAYAAJ.

Love, D. A. (2007). *The color of law on the pope, paternalism and purifying the savages.* Retrieved from UMD edu/CD/Religion/love.Pdf.

Mannoni, O. (1962). *Prospero and Caliban: The psychology of colonization.* New York: Praeger.

McGarrity, G. & Cardenas, O. (1995). Cuba in *Afro-Latin Americans today: No longer invisible.* (pp. 77-108). London: Minority Rights Group, Minority Rights Group publications.

Morgan, K. (1993). *Bristol and the Atlantic trade in the eighteenth century.* Cambridge: Cambridge University Press.

Morison, S. (1972). *The Oxford history of the American people.* New York, NY: Mentor.

Mphahlele, E. (1987). "Images of the African personality." Paper presented at Conference on Black Culture and Business, Johannesburg.

Muhammad, J. (1995). Mexico and Central America: Mexico in *Afro-Latin Americans today: No longer invisible.* (pp. 163-180). London, UK: Minority Rights Group, Minority Rights Group publications.

Myers, L. (1988). *Understanding an Afrocentric worldview.* DuBuque, IA: Kendall/Hall.

Nascimento, A. (1979). *Brazil mixture or massacre?: Essays in the genocide of a Black people.* Dover, MA: The Majority Press.

Nascimento, A., Nascimento, E., & Nascimento, A. (1992). *Africans in Brazil: A Pan-African perspective.* Trenton, NJ: African World Press.

Nobles, W. (1972). African philosophy: Foundations for Black psychology In R. Jones (2nd Ed.). *Black psychology.* (pp. 47-64). New York: Harper & Row.

Nobles, W., Khatib, S. (Clark, C.), McGee, D., & Akbar, N. (1975). Voodoo or I.Q.: An introduction to African psychology. *Journal of Black Psychology.* 1(2), 1-20.

Nobles, W., King, L., & Dixon, V. (1976). *African philosophy: Assumptions and paradigms for research on black people.* Los Angeles: Fanon Center Publications.

Nobles, W. (1974). African root and American fruit: The Black family in W. Nobles *Seeking the sakhu: foundational writings for an African psychology.* (pp. 131-144). Chicago: Third World Press.

Nobles, W. (1994). Implementing our international agenda: Step 1. *Psychological Discourse,* 25, 4-5.

Nobles, W. (1985). *Africanity and the Black Family: The Development of a Theoretical Model.* Oakland, CA: A Black Family Institute Publication.

Nobles, W. (1986a). *African psychology: Toward its reclamation, reascension and revitalization.* Oakland, CA: A Black Family Institute Publication.

Nobles, W. (1986b). Ancient Egyptian thought and the renaissance of African (Black) psychology. In M. Karenga, & J. Carruthers, (Eds.) *Kemet and the African worldview.* Los Angeles: University of Sankore Press.

Nobles, W. (1997). To be African or not to be: The question of identity or authenticity – some preliminary thoughts. In W. Nobles *Seeking the sakhu: foundational writings for an African Psychology.* (pp. 317-340). Chicago: Third World Press.

Nobles, W. (2003). Reparations and health care for African Americans: Repairing the damage from the legacy of slavery. In R. Winbush (Ed.), *Should America pay? Slavery and the raging debate on reparations.* New York: Amistad Press.

Nobles, W. (2005). Maroon societies. In M. Asante & M. Mazama (Eds.). *Encyclopedia of Black studies.* Thousand Oaks, CA: SAGE Publications.

Nobles, W. (2008). *Shattered consciousness & fractured identity: The lingering psychological effects of the transatlantic slave trade experience.* Chicago: The Illinois Transatlantic Slave Trade Commission.

Ortner, S. (1973). On key symbols. *American Anthropologists,* 75(5), 1335-46.

Parham, T. (1989). Cycles of psychological nigrescence. *The Counseling Psychologist,* 17 (2), 187-226.

Perimbaum, B. (1982). *Holy violence: The revolutionary thought of Frantz Fanon.* Washington, D.C. Three Continents Press.

Philip P. & Yankah, K. *African folklore: an encyclopedia.* New York: Routledge

Piper-Mandy, E. & Rowe, T. (2010). Educating African-centered psychologists: Towards a comprehensive paradigm. *Journal of Pan-African Studies,* 3(8), 5-23.

Rainsford, M. (1805). *An Historical Account of the Black Empire of Hayti: comprehending a view of the principal transactions in the revolution of Saint Domingo.* Albion Press printed, published by James Cundee, Ivy-Lane, Paternoster-Row. C. Chapple, Fall Mall.

Rééd, M. Bazile, TBD & Madiou, T. (1989) *L'Histoire d'Haïti.* Port-au-Prince, Haiti: Editions Henri Deschamps. (8 Volumes; Original published in 1847,http://thelouvertureproject. org/index. php?title=D%C3%A9d%C3%A9e_Bazile).

Riesman, B. (2011) *I Feel so good: The life and times of Big Bill Broonzy.* Chicago: University of Chicago Press.

Rodriguez, J. (2007). *Encyclopedia of slave resistance and rebellion.* (Vol. 2). Westport, CT: Greenwood Publishing Group.

Sansone, L., Soumonni, E. & Boubacar B. (Eds.). (2008). *Africa, Brazil and the construction of Transatlantic Black Identities.* Trenton, NJ: African World Press.

Semaj, L. (1981). The Black self: identity and models for psychological liberation. *Western Journal of Black Studies,* 5(3), 158-171.

Shivji, I. (2009). *Nyerere's nationalist legacy.* Retrieved from: http://pambazuka.org/en/category/panafrican/6070.

Stovall, T. (2006). "Race and the Making of the Nation: Blacks in Modern France." In Michael A. Gomez (Ed.). *Diasporic Africa: A reader.* New York: New York University Press.

Thompson, A. (2006). *Flight to freedom: African runaways and Maroons in America.* University of West Indies Press, Jamaica.

Thornton, J. (1993). I am the subject of the king of Congo: African political ideology and the Haitian revolution. *Journal of World History,* 4(2), 181-214.

Vander, J. and Mahlon, B. (1928). *Black majesty: the life of Christophe, king of Haiti.* New York, NY: Harper and Brothers Publishing.

Vandercook, C. (2007). *The armorial of Haiti: Symbols of nobility in the reign of Henry Christophe.* London: The College of Arms.

Verzijl, J., Heere, W. & Offerhaus, J. (1979). *International law in historical perspective.* Cambridge, MA: Martinus Nijhoff Publishers.

Vieira, R. (1995). Brazil in *Afro-Latin Americans today: No longer invisible.* (pp. 19-46). London, UK: Minority Rights Group, Minority Rights Group publications.

Walker, S. (Ed.). (2001). *African roots/American culture: Africa in the creation of the Americas.* NY: Rowman & Littlefield Publishers, Inc.

Weaver, K. (2006). *Medical revolutionaries: The enslaved healers of eighteenth-century Saint-Domingue.* Urbana, IL: University of Illinois Press.

Willem. J. H. and W.P. Heere, (1997) Offerhaus International Law in Historical Perspective Online, Google Books. http://books.google.com/books?id=5kTneDFadclC.

Wilson, A. (1993). *The falsification of Afrikan consciousness: Euro-centric history, psychiatry and the politics of white supremacy.* Bronx, NY: Afrikan World InfoSystems.

Wilson, S. (1990). *Hispaniola - Caribbean chiefdoms in the age of Columbus.* Tuscaloosa, AL: The University of Alabama Press.

Winbush, R. (2003). *Should America pay? slavery and the raging debate on reparations.* New York: Amistad Press.

Woodson, Carter Godwin (1990). *The Mis-education of the Negro.* Trenton, N.J: Africa World Press.

Wright, Bobby (1979). *Mentacide: The ultimate threat to the Black race.* unpublished manuscript.

Appendix 1:

The Bull *Inter Caetera* (Alexander VI), May 4, 1493.

Alexander, bishop, servant of the servants of God, to the illustrious sovereigns, our very dear son in Christ, Ferdinand, king, and our very dear daughter in Christ, Isabella, queen of Castile, Leon, Aragon, Sicily, and Granada, health and apostolic benediction. Among other works well pleasing to the Divine Majesty and cherished of our heart, this assuredly ranks highest, that in our times especially the Catholic faith and the Christian religion be exalted and be everywhere increased and spread, that the health of souls be cared for and that barbarous nations be overthrown and brought to the faith itself. Wherefore inasmuch as by the favor of divine clemency, we, though of insufficient merits, have been called to this Holy See of Peter, recognizing that as true Catholic kings and princes, such as we have known you always to be, and as your illustrious deeds already known to almost the whole world declare, you not only eagerly desire but with every effort, zeal, and diligence, without regard to hardships, expenses, dangers, with the shedding even of your blood, are laboring to that end; recognizing also that you have long since dedicated to this purpose your whole soul and all your endeavors -- as witnessed in these times with so much glory to the Divine Name in your recovery of the kingdom of Granada from the yoke of the Saracens -- we therefore are rightly led, and hold it as our duty, to grant you even of our own accord and in your favor those things whereby with effort each day more hearty you may be enabled for the honor of God himself and the spread of the Christian rule to carry forward your holy and praiseworthy purpose so pleasing to immortal God. We have indeed learned that you, who for a long time had intended to seek out and discover certain islands and mainlands remote and unknown and not hitherto discovered by others, to the end that you might bring to the worship of our Redeemer and the profession of the Catholic faith their residents and inhabitants, having been up to the present time greatly engaged in the siege and recovery of the kingdom itself of Granada were unable to accomplish this holy and praiseworthy purpose; but the said kingdom having at length been regained, as was pleasing to the Lord, you, with the wish to fulfill your desire, chose our beloved son, Christopher Columbus, a man assuredly worthy and of the highest recommendations and fitted for so great an undertaking, whom you furnished with ships and men equipped for like designs, not without the greatest hardships, dangers, and expenses, to make diligent quest for these remote and unknown mainlands and islands through the sea, where hitherto no one had sailed; and they at length, with divine aid and with the utmost diligence sailing in the ocean sea, discovered certain very remote islands and even mainlands that hitherto had not been discovered by others; wherein dwell very many peoples living in peace, and, as reported, going unclothed, and not eating flesh. Moreover, as your aforesaid envoys are of opinion, these very peoples living in the said islands and countries believe in one God, the Creator in heaven, and seem sufficiently disposed to embrace the Catholic faith and be trained in good morals. And it is hoped that, were they instructed, the name of the Savior, our Lord Jesus Christ, would easily be introduced into the said countries and islands. Also, on one of the chief of these aforesaid islands the said Christopher has already caused to be put together and built a fortress fairly equipped, wherein he has stationed as garrison certain Christians, companions of his, who are to make search for other remote and unknown islands and mainlands. In the islands and countries already discovered are found gold, spices, and very many other precious things of divers kinds and qualities. Wherefore, as becomes Catholic kings and princes, after earnest consideration of all matters, especially of the rise and spread of the Catholic faith, as was the fashion of your ancestors, kings of renowned memory, you have purposed with the favor of divine clemency to bring under your sway the said mainlands and islands with their residents and inhabitants and to bring

them to the Catholic faith. Hence, heartily commending in the
Lord this your holy and praiseworthy purpose, and desirous
that it be duly accomplished, and that the name of our Savior
be carried into those regions, we exhort you very earnestly in
the Lord and by your reception of holy baptism, whereby you
are bound to our apostolic commands, and by the bowels of
the mercy of our Lord Jesus Christ, enjoin strictly, that inasmuch as with eager zeal for the true faith you design to equip
and despatch this expedition, you purpose also, as is your
duty, to lead the peoples dwelling in those islands and countries to embrace the Christian religion; nor at any time let
dangers or hardships deter you therefrom, with the stout
hope and trust in your hearts that Almighty God will further
your undertakings. And, in order that you may enter upon so
great an undertaking with greater readiness and heartiness
endowed with the benefit of our apostolic favor, we, of our
own accord, not at your instance nor the request of anyone
else in your regard, but of our own sole largess and certain
knowledge and out of the fullness of our apostolic power, by
the authority of Almighty God conferred upon us in blessed
Peter and of the vicarship of Jesus Christ, which we hold on
earth, do by tenor of these presents, should any of said
islands have been found by your envoys and captains, give,
grant, and assign to you and your heirs and successors,
kings of Castile and Leon, forever, together with all their
dominions, cities, camps, places, and villages, and all rights,
jurisdictions, and appurtenances, all islands and mainlands
found and to be found, discovered and to be discovered
towards the west and south, by drawing and establishing a
line from the Arctic pole, namely the north, to the Antarctic
pole, namely the south, no matter whether the said mainlands and islands are found and to be found in the direction
of India or towards any other quarter, the said line to be distant one hundred leagues towards the west and south from
any of the islands commonly known as the Azores and Cape
Verde. With this proviso however that none of the islands

and mainlands, found and to be found, discovered and to be discovered, beyond that said line towards the west and south, be in the actual possession of any Christian king or prince up to the birthday of our Lord Jesus Christ just past from which the present year one thousand four hundred and ninety-three begins. And we make, appoint, and depute you and your said heirs and successors lords of them with full and free power, authority, and jurisdiction of every kind; with this proviso however, that by this our gift, grant, and assignment no right acquired by any Christian prince, who may be in actual possession of said islands and mainlands prior to the said birthday of our Lord Jesus Christ, is hereby to be understood to be withdrawn or taken away. Moreover we command you in virtue of holy obedience that, employing all due diligence in the premises, as you also promise -- nor do we doubt your compliance therein in accordance with your loyalty and royal greatness of spirit -- you should appoint to the aforesaid mainlands and islands worthy, God-fearing, learned, skilled, and experienced men, in order to instruct the aforesaid inhabitants and residents in the Catholic faith and train them in good morals. Furthermore, under penalty of excommunication *late sententie* to be incurred *ipso facto*, should anyone thus contravene, we strictly forbid all persons of whatsoever rank, even imperial and royal, or of whatsoever estate, degree, order, or condition, to dare, without your special permit or that of your aforesaid heirs and successors, to go for the purpose of trade or any other reason to the islands or mainlands, found and to be found, discovered and to be discovered, towards the west and south, by drawing and establishing a line from the Arctic pole to the Antarctic pole, no matter whether the mainlands and islands, found and to be found, lie in the direction of India or toward any other quarter whatsoever, the said line to be distant one hundred leagues towards the west and south, as is aforesaid, from any of the islands commonly known as the Azores and Cape Verde; apostolic constitutions and ordinances and other decrees whatsoever to the contrary notwithstanding. We trust in Him from whom empires and governments and all good things proceed, that, should you, with the Lord's guidance, pursue this holy and praiseworthy undertaking, in a short while your hardships and endeavors will attain the most felicitous result, to the happiness and glory of all Christendom. But inasmuch as it would be difficult to have these present letters sent to all places where desirable, we wish, and with similar accord and knowledge do decree, that to copies of them, signed by the hand of a public notary commissioned therefor, and sealed with the seal of any ecclesiastical officer or ecclesiastical court, the same respect is to be shown in court and outside as well as anywhere else as would be given to these presents should they thus be exhibited or shown. Let no one, therefore, infringe, or with rash boldness contravene, this our recommendation, exhortation, requisition, gift, grant, assignment, constitution, deputation, decree, mandate, prohibition, and will. Should anyone presume to attempt this, be it known to him that he will incur the wrath of Almighty God and of the blessed apostles Peter and Paul. Given at Rome, at St. Peter's, in the year of the incarnation of our Lord one thousand four hundred and ninety-three, the fourth of May, and the first year of our pontificate. Gratis by order of our most holy lord, the pope.

Appendix 2:

CONSTITUTION OF 1801

The representatives of the colony of Saint-Domingue, gathered in Central Assembly, have arrested and established the constitutional bases of the regime of the French colony of Saint-Domingue as follows:

TITLE I
Of the Territory
Art. 1.
Saint-Domingue in its entire expanse, and Samana, La Tortue, La Gonâve, Les Cayemites, L'Ile-à-Vache, La Saône and other adjacent islands form the territory of a single colony, which is part of the French Empire, but ruled under particular laws.

Art. 2.
The territory of this colony is divided in departments, districts (arrondissements) and parishes.

TITLE II
Of the Inhabitants
Art. 3.
There cannot exist slaves on this territory, servitude is therein forever abolished. All men are born, live and die free and French.

Art. 4.
All men, regardless of color, are eligible to all employment.

Art. 5.
There shall exist no distinction other than those based on virtue and talent, and other superiority afforded by law in the exercise of a public function. The law is the same for all whether in punishment or in protection.

TITLE III
Of the Religion
Art. 6.
The catholic, apostolic, Roman faith shall be the only publicly professed faith.

Art. 7.
Each parish shall provide to the maintaining of religious

cult and of its ministers. The wealth of the factories shall be especially allocated to this expense, and the presbyteries to the housing of ministers.

Art. 8.

The governor of the colony shall assign to each minister of the religion the extent of his spiritual administration, and said ministers can never, under any circumstance, form a corps in the colony.

TITLE IV
Of the Mores
Art. 9.

Marriage, by its civic and religious institution, tend to the purity of mores; spouses who will practice the virtues required by their condition shall always be distinguished and especially protected by the government.

Art. 10.

Divorce shall not take place in the colony.

Art. 11.

Laws that will tend to expand and maintain social virtues, and to encourage and cement family bonding shall fix condition and rights of children born in wedlock.

TITLE V
Of Men in Society
Art. 12.

The Constitution guarantees freedom and individual security. No one shall be arrested unless a formally expressed mandate, issued from a functionary to whom the law grants the right to order arrest and detention in a publicly designated location.

Art. 13.

Property is sacred and inviolable. All people, either by himself, or by his representatives, has the free right to dispose and to administer property that is recognized as belonging to him. Anyone who attempts to deny this right shall become guilty of crime towards society and responsible towards the person troubled in his property.

TITLE VI
Of Cultures and Commerce
Art. 14.
The colony being essentially agricultural cannot suffer the least disruption in the works of its cultivation.
Art. 15.
Each habitation shall constitute a manufacture that requires the gathering of cultivators and workers; it shall represent the quiet haven of an active and constant family, of which the owner of the land or his representative shall be the father.
Art. 16.
Each cultivator and each worker is a member of the family and shares in parts of the revenues. Every change in domicile on the part of the cultivator carries the ruin of the cultivation. In order to repress a vice as disruptive to the colony as it is to public order, the governor issues all policy requirements necessary in the circumstances and in conformance with the bases of the rules of policy[1] of 20 Vendémiaire, year IX,[2] and of the proclamation of the following I9 Pluviôse[3] of the Chief General Toussaint-Louverture.
Art. 17.
The introduction of cultivators indispensable to the reestablishment and to the growth of agriculture shall take place in Saint-Domingue. The Constitution charges the Governor to take convenient measures to encourage and favor the increase in manpower, to stipulate and balance the diverse interests, to ensure and guarantee the execution of respective engagements resulting from this introduction.
Art. 18.
Commerce in the colony consists solely of the exchange of foodstuffs and products of its territory;[4] consequently, the introduction of goods similar in nature is and shall remains prohibited.
TITLE VII
Of the Legislation and Legislative Authority
Art 19.

The colonial regime is determined by laws proposed by the
Governor and rendered by a gathering of inhabitants, who
shall meet at fixed periods at the central seat of the colony
under the title Central Assembly of Saint-Domingue.
Art. 20.
No law relative to the internal administration of the colony
shall be promulgated unless it contain the following formula:
The Central Assembly of Saint-Domingue, upon the proposition of the Governor, renders the following law:
Art. 21.
No law shall be obligatory to the citizen until the day it is
promulgated in the chief town of departments. The promulgation of law shall take place as follows: In the name[5] of the
French colony of Saint-Domingue, the Governor orders that
the subsequent law be sealed, promulgated and executed in
all of the colony.
Art. 22.
The Central Assembly of Saint-Domingue shall be composed
of two representatives of department, whom, to be eligible,
shall be at least 30 years of age and have resided for 5
years in the colony.
Art. 23.
The Assembly shall be renewed every two years by half; no
one shall be a member for six consecutive years. The election shall proceed as follows: municipal administrations nominate every two years, on 10 Ventôse[6] each of the deputies,
whom shall meet ten days thereafter at the chief town of
their respective departments, where they shall form as many
departmental electoral assemblies that will nominate, each,
one representative to the Central Assembly. The next election shall take place on the 10th Ventôse of the eleventh year
of the French Republic.[7] In case of death, resignation or
other vacancy of one or several members of the Assembly,
the Governor shall provide a replacement. He shall equally
designate the members of the actual Central Assembly who,
at the time of first renewal, shall remain members of the

Assembly for two additional years.
Art. 24.
The Central Assembly shall vote the adoption or the rejection of laws that are proposed to it by the Governor; it shall express its vote on rules made and on the application of laws already made, on abuses to correct, on improvements to undertake in all parts of service of the colony.
Art. 25.
The session shall begin each year on the 1st of Germinal[8] and shall not exceed three months in duration. The Governor can convoke the Assembly in extraordinary meeting; the hearings shall not be public.
Art. 26.
On the state of revenues and spending that are proposed to the Assembly by the Governor, the Central Assembly shall determine, when appropriate, establishment of rates, quotas, the duration and mode of tax collection, its increase or decrease; these conditions shall be summarily printed.
TITLE VIII
Of the Government
Art. 27.
The administrative direction of the government shall be entrusted to a Governor who corresponds directly with the government of the Metropole, on all matters relative to the interests of the colony.
Art. 28.
The Constitution nominates the citizen Toussaint-Louverture, Chief General of the army of Saint-Domingue, and, in consideration for important services rendered to the colony, in the most critical circumstances of the revolution, and upon the wishes of the grateful inhabitants, he is entrusted the direction thereof for the remainder of his glorious life.
Art. 29.
In the future, each governor shall be nominated for five years, and shall continue every five years for reasons of his good administration.

Art. 30.
In order to strengthen the tranquility that the colony owes to steadfastness, activity, indefatigable zeal and rare virtues of the General Toussaint-Louverture, and in sign of the unlimited trust of the inhabitants of Saint-Domingue, the Constitution attribute exclusively to this general the right to designate the citizen who, in the unfortunate event of the general's death, shall immediately replace him. This choice shall remain secret; it shall be cosigned under sealed envelope and to be opened only by the Central Assembly, in presence of all active generals and chief commanders of departments of the army of Saint-Domingue. The Governor Toussaint-Louverture shall take all necessary precautionary measures to let the Central Assembly know the depository of this important envelope.

Art. 31.
The citizen that shall be chosen by Governor Toussaint-Louverture to take the direction of the government upon his death, shall swear in front of the Central Assembly to execute the Constitution of Saint-Domingue and to remain attached to the French government, and shall be immediately installed in his functions; all shall be in presence of active generals and chief commanders of departments of the army of Saint-Domingue, who all, individually and without delay, shall swear obedience to the orders of the new governor.[9]

Art. 32.
At least one month before the expiration of the five years fixed for the administration of each General, the one in central function, jointly with the active-duty Generals and Chief Commanders of Departments, shall meet at the ordinary place of hearing of the Central Assembly. to the effect of nominating, concurrently with the members of this Assembly, the new Governor or continue the administration of the one who is in function.

Art. 33.
Failure on the part of a Governor in function to convoke constitutes a manifest infraction to the Constitution. In such circumstance, the highest ranked General or the senior General of equal rank, who is in active service in the colony, shall take, of right, if provisionally, the control the govermnent. This General shall convoke immediately the other General in active duty, the Chief Commanders of Departments and the members of the Central Assembly, who shall all obey the convocation, to the effect of proceeding concurrently to the nomination of a new Governor. In the event of death, resignation or other vacancy by a Governor before the expiration of his mandate, the Government passes as well provisionally to the highest ranked General, or the senior General of equal rank who shall convoke, to the same ends as above, the members of the Central Assembly, the active-duty Generals and Chief Commanders of Departments.

Art. 34.
The Governor shall seal and promulgate the laws; he nominates to all civilian and military employment. He is the chief commander of the armed forces and is charged with its organization; State vessels in station at the shores of the colony receive orders from him. He shall determine the divisions of the territory in manners most conform to internal relations. He watches and provides, according to the law, for internal and external security of the colony, and given that the state of war is a state of abandonment, malaise and nullity for the colony, the Governor is charged to take in those circumstances measures he deems necessary to ensure the subsistence and the supply of goods of all sorts to the colony.

Art. 35.
He shall exercise the general policy[10] of inhabitants and of the factories, and enforce the obligations of owners, farmers and of their representatives towards cultivators and workers, and the duty of cultivators towards owners, farmers or their representatives.

Art. 36.
He shall propose laws to the Central Assembly, as well as changes to the Constitution that experience may necessitate.
Art. 37.
He shall direct, supervise the collection, the payments and the use of finances of the colony, and shall give, to this effect, any and all orders.
Art. 38.
He shall present, every two years, to the Central Assembly the conditions of receipts and disbursements of each department, year by year.
Art. 39.
He shall supervise and censor by the authority of his commissaries, all writings designed for printing on the island he shall cause to be suppressed all those coming from abroad that would tend to corrupt mores or trouble the new colony; he shall punish the authors or colporteurs, according to the severity of the situation.
Art. 40.
If the Governor is informed of some plot against the tranquility of the colony, he shall immediately proceed to the arrest of the presumed authors, instigators or accomplices; after having them undergo extra-judiciary questioning, he shall cite them in front of a competent tribunal.
Art. 41.
The salary of the Governor is fixed at the present time at 300,000 Francs. His honor guard shall be charged to the colony.
TITLE IX
Of the Courts
Art. 42.
Citizens shall have an inalienable right to be judged by arbiters at their choice.
Art. 43.
No authority shall suspend nor impeach the execution of judgments rendered by the Courts.

Art. 44.

Justice shall be administered in the colony by Courts of first instance and by Courts of appeal. The law determines their organization, their number, their competence and the territory of each Courtís jurisdiction. These tribunals, according to their degree of jurisdiction, shall recognize all civil and criminal affairs.

Art. 45.

There shall exist for the colony a Court of Cassation that shall pronounce on demands of annulments against judgments rendered by Appeal Courts, and issue opinions against an entire tribunal. This court does not hear the facts of the cases, but overturns judgments rendered on procedures in which the forms have been violated; or that contain some express contravention of the law, and shall return the facts of the process to the tribunal in question.

Art. 46.

Judges of divers Courts conserve their function for life, unless they are condemned for abuse of authority.[11] Commissaries of the government can be revoked.

Art. 47.

Military misdemeanors shall be submitted to special tribunals and subject to special judgments. These special Courts also hear cases of theft, abduction, domicile violation, murder, assassination, arson, rape, plotting and mutiny. The organization of these Courts pertains to the Governor of the colony.

TITLE X
Of Municipal Administrations

Art. 48.

There shall be in each parish of the colony a municipal administration; where there is a Court of first instance, the administrative body shall be composed of a mayor and four administrators. The commissary of the government near the tribunal shall hold gratuitously the functions of commissary near the municipal administration. In other parishes, municipal administrations shall be composed of a mayor and

two administrators; a substitute commissary of the responsible tribunal shall hold the function of commissary near the
municipality gratuitously.

Art. 49.

Members of these municipal administrations shall be nominated for two years; they may always continue beyond that
time. Their nomination devolves to the Governor, who, on a
list of at least sixteen individuals, presented by each municipal administration, chooses the persons most appropriate to
manage the affairs of each parish.

Art. 50.

The function of municipal administrators consists in the exercise of simple policy[12] of cities and towns, in the administration of taxes originating from revenues of factories[13] and
additional impositions of the parishes. They are, in addition,
especially charged with the record keeping of births, marriages and deaths.

Art. 51.

The mayors exert particular functions that the law determines.

TITLE XI

Of the Armed Forces

Art. 52.

The Armed Forces are essentially obedient, they can never
deliberate; they are at the disposition of the Governor who
can mobilize them only to maintain public order, protection
due to all citizens, and the defense of the colony.

Art. 53.

They are divided in paid colonial guard and unpaid colonial
guard.

Art. 54.

The unpaid colonial guard shall not go out of the limits of its
parish unless there is a case of imminent danger, and upon
the order and the responsibility of the local military commander. Outside of its parish it shall be compensated; and

shall be submitted, in this case, to military discipline, and in all other case, is only subject to the law.

Art. 55.

The state police force of the colony shall be part of the Armed Forces; it shall be divided in a mounted force and a pedestrian force. The mounted force is instituted for the high police of security of the countryside; it has the charge of the wealth of the colony. The pedestrian force is instituted as the police of cities and towns; it shall be at the charge of the city or town for which it performs services.

Art. 56.

The army is recruited upon the proposition the Governor makes to the Central Assembly, according to the mode established by law.

TITLE XII

Of Finances, of Sequestered and Vacant Estates

Art. 57.

The finances of the colony shall be composed of: 1) duties on imports, weights and measures; 2) duties on the rental value of city and town houses, and duties on manufactured goods, other than agriculture and salt marshes; 3) revenues from ferries and postal services; 4) fines and confiscated wrecks; 5) duties on rescue of wrecked ships; revenue of colonial domains.

Art. 58.

The product of fermage[14] from sequestered properties of absentee and unrepresented[15] owners becomes provisionally part of the public revenue of the colony and shall be applied to expenses of administration. The circumstances shall determine the laws that should be made relative to outstanding public debt, and to farming of sequestered property collected by the administration prior to the promulgation of the present law.

Art. 59.

Funds originating from the sales of personal estates and from the price of fermage of vacant inheritances opened in the colony under the French government since 1789, as well as real estate gathered under colonial domains, shall be placed in a particular coffer, and shall not be available, until two years after the publication of peace in the island, between France and the maritime powers; let it be understood, that this deadline is only relative to inheritances whose five year deadline fixed by the edict of 1781 should expire; and concerning those opened on or around the peace period, they shall not become available and gathered until after seven years.

Art. 60.

Foreign successors of French parents or foreign parents in France shall succeed them also in Saint-Domingue; they shall be allowed to enter contract, acquire and receive properties situated in the colony, and dispose as well as the French by all means authorized by laws.

Art. 61.

Laws shall determine the mode of collection of the administration of finances and sequestered vacant estates.

Art. 62.

A temporary commission of accounting shall regulate and verify the revenue and disbursement accounts of the colony; this commission shall consist of three members, chosen and nominated by the Governor.

TITLE XIII

General Dispositions

Art. 63.

The residence of any person shall constitute an inviolable asylum.[16] During nighttime, no one shall have the right to enter therein unless in case of fire, flooding or upon request from within. During the day, one shall have access for a special determined object or, by a law, or by order issued from a public authority.

Art. 64.

For a lawful arrest to be executed; it must: 1) formally express the motive of the arrest and the law in virtue of which it is ordered; 2) be issued from a functionary whom the law formally empowers to do so; 3) be presented to the person in form of copy of the warrant.

Art. 65.

Anyone who, without authority of the law to make an arrest, gives, signs, executes or causes to be executed the arrest of a person, shall be guilty of the crime of arbitrary detention.

Art. 66.

Any person shall have the right to address individual petitions to all constitutional authority and especially to the Governor.

Art. 67.

There cannot exist in the colony corporations or associations that are contrary to public order. No citizen association shall be qualified as popular society. All seditious gathering shall be dissipated immediately, first by way of verbal order and, if necessary, by development of armed force.

Art. 68.

Any person shall have the faculty to form particular establishments of education and instruction for the youth under the authorization and the supervision of municipal administrations.

Art. 69.

The law supervises especially all professions dealing with public mores, public safety, health and fortune of citizens.

Art. 70.

The law provides for awards to inventors of rural machines, or for the preservation of the exclusive ownership of their discoveries.

Art. 71.

There shall exist in the colony uniformity of weights and measures.

Art. 72.

It shall be given, by the Governor, in the name of the colony, awards to warriors who will have rendered exceptional services while fighting for the common defense.

Art. 73.

Absentee owners, for whatever reason, conserve all their rights to properties belonging to them and situated in the colony; it suffices, to remove any sequestration that might have been imposed, to reintroduce their titles of ownership and; in default of title thereof, supplementary acts whose formula is determined by law. Exempt of this disposition are, nevertheless, those who might been inscribed and maintained on the general list of emigrants of France; their properties shall continue, in this case, to be administered as colonial domains until their removal from the list.

Art. 74.

The colony proclaims, as guarantee of public law, that all leases of properties legally leased by the administration shall have their full effect, if the contracting parties prefer not to compromise with owners or their representatives who would obtain the return of their sequestered goods.

Art. 75.

It proclaims that it is on the respect of persons and properties that rest agriculture, all productions, all means of employment and all social order.

Art. 76.

It proclaims that any citizen owes services to the land that nourishes him or that guarantees his rights, and in regard to those [services] that shall have been collected, at a later time, they shall be exactable and reimbursed in the year that follows the lifting of sequestration of goods.

Art. 77.

The Chief General Toussaint-Louverture is and shall remain charged with sending the present Constitution to be sanctioned by the French government; nevertheless, and given the absence of laws, the urgency to exit from this condition of peril, the necessity to promptly reestablish agriculture and the unanimous wishes pronounced by the inhabitants of Saint-Domingue, the Chief General is and remains invited, in the name of public good, to proceed with its execution in all areas of the territory of the colony.

Made at Port-Republican,[17]] this 19 Floréal year IX[18] of the French Republic, one and indivisible.

Signed: Borgella, *President*, Raymond, Collet, Gaston Nogérée, Lacour, Roxas, Muñoz, Mancebo, E. Viart,[19] *secretary.*

After having taken knowledge of the Constitution, I give it my approval. The invitation of the Central Assembly is for me an order; consequently, I shall pass it to the French government in order to obtain its sanction; as for its execution in the colony, the wish expressed by the Central Assembly shall be fulfilled as well and executed. Given at Cap Français,[20] this 14 Messidor, year IX[21] of the French Republic, one and indivisible.

The Chief General:
Signed: TOUSSAINT-LOUVERTURE

Appendix 3:

THE 1805 CONSTITUTION OF HAITI

SECOND CONSTITUTION OF HAITI (HAYTI) MAY 20, 1805. PROMULGATED BY EMPEROR JACQUES I (DESSALINES)

The document below was printed in the New York Evening Post, July 15, 1805.

=================

CONSTITUTION OF HAYTI

We, H. Christophe, Clerveaux, Vernet, Gabart, Petion, Geffard, Toussaint, Brave, Raphael, Roamin, Lalondridie, Capoix, Magny, Daut, Conge, Magloire, Ambrose, Yayou, Jean Louis Franchois, Gerin, Mereau, Fervu, Bavelais, Martial Besse...

As well in our name as in that of the people of Hayti, who have legally constituted us faithfully organs and interpreters of their will, in presence of the Supreme Being, before whom all mankind are equal, and who has scattered so many species of creatures on the surface of the earth for the purpose of manifesting his glory and his power by the diversity of his works, in the presence of all nature by whom we have been so unjustly and for so long a time considered as outcast children.

Do declare that the tenor of the present constitution is the free spontaneous and invariable expression of our hearts, and the general will of our constituents, and we submit it to the sanction of H.M. the Emperor Jacques Dessalines our deliverer, to receive its speedy and entire execution.

Preliminary Declaration.

Art. 1. The people inhabiting the island formerly called St. Domingo, hereby agree to form themselves into a free state sovereign and independent of any other power in the universe, under the name of empire of Hayti.

2. Slavery is forever abolished.

3. The Citizens of Hayti are brothers at home; equality in the eyes of the law is incontestably

acknowledged, and there cannot exist any titles, advantages, or privileges, other than those necessarily resulting from the

213

consideration and reward of services rendered to liberty and independence.

4. The law is the same to all, whether it punishes, or whether it protects.

5. The law has no retroactive effect.

6. Property is sacred, its violation shall be severely prosecuted.

7. The quality of citizen of Hayti is lost by emigration and naturalization in foreign countries and condemnation to corporal or disgrace punishments. The fist case carries with it the punishment of death and confiscation of property.

8. The quality of Citizen is suspended in consequence of bankruptcies and failures.

9. No person is worth of being a Haitian who is not a good father, good son, a good husband, and especially a good soldier.

10. Fathers and mothers are not permitted to disinherit their children.

11. Every Citizen must possess a mechanic art.

12. No whiteman of whatever nation he may be, shall put his foot on this territory with the title of master or proprietor, neither shall he in future acquire any property therein.

13. The preceding article cannot in the smallest degree affect white woman who have been naturalized Haytians by Government, nor does it extend to children already born, or that may be born of the said women. The Germans and Polanders naturalized by government are also comprized (sic) in the dispositions of the present article.

14. All acception (sic) of colour among the children of one and the same family, of whom the chief magistrate is the father, being necessarily to cease, the Haytians shall hence forward be known only by the generic appellation of Blacks.

Of the Empire

15. The Empire of Hayti is one and indivisible. Its territory is distributed into six military divisions.

16. Each military division shall be commanded by a general of division.

17. These generals of division shall be independent of one another, and shall correspond directly with the Emperor, or with the general in chief appointed by his Majesty.

18. The following Islands are integral parts of the Empire, viz. Samana, La Tortue, La Gonave, Les Cayemites, La Saone, L'Isle a Vache, and other adjacent islands.

Of the Government

19. The Government of Hayti is entrusted to a first Magistrate, who assumes the title of Emperor and commander in chief of the army.

20. The people acknowledge for Emperor and Commander in Chief of the Army, Jacques Dessalines, the avenger and deliverer of his fellow citizens. The title of Majesty is conferred upon him, as well as upon his august spouse, the Empress.

21. The person of their Majesties are sacred and inviolable.

22. The State will appropriate a fixed annual allowance to her Majesty the Empress, which she will continue to enjoy even after the decease of the Emperor, as princess dowager.

23. The crown is elective not hereditary.

24. There shall be assigned by the state an annual income to the children acknowledge by his Majesty the Emperor.

25. The male children acknowledged by the Emperor shall be obliged, in the same manner as other citizens, to pass successively from grade to grade, with this only difference, that their entrance into service shall begin at the fourth demi brigade, from the period of their birth.

26. The Emperor designates, in the manner he may judge expedient, the person who is to be his successor either before or after his death.

27. A suitable provision shall be made by the state to that successor from the moment of his accession to the throne.

28. The Emperor, and his successors, shall in no case and under no pretext whatsoever, have the right of attacking to their persons any particular or privileged body, whether as guards of honour, or under any other denomination.

29. Every successor deviating from the dispositions of the preceding article, or from the principles consecrated in the present constitution shall be considered and declared in a state of warfare against the society. In such a case, the counselors of state will assemble in order to pronounce his removal, and to chose one among themselves who shall be judged the most worthy of replacing him; and if it should happen that the said successor oppose the execution of this measure, authorized by law, the Generals, counselor of state, shall appeal to the people and the army, who will immediately give their whole strength and assistance to maintain Liberty.

30. The Emperor makes seals and promulgates the laws; appoints and revokes at will, the Ministers, the General in Chief for the Army, the Counselors of State, the Generals and other agents of the Empire, the sea offices, the members of the local administrations, the Commissaries of Government near the Tribunals, the judges, and other public functionaries.

31. The Emperor directs the receipts and expenditures of the State, Surveys the Mint of which he alone orders the emission, and fixes the weight and the model.

32. To him alone is reserved the power of making peace or war, to maintain political intercourse, and to form treaties.

33. He provides for the interior safety and for the defense of the State: and distributes at pleasure the sea and land forces.

34. In case of conspiracies manifesting themselves against the safety of the state, against the constitution, or against his person, the Emperor shall cause the authors or accomplices to be arrested and tried before a special Council.

35. His Majesty has alone the right to absolve a criminal and commute his punishment.

36. The Emperor shall never form any enterprize (sic) with the views of making conquests, nor to disturb the peace and interior administration of foreign colonies.

37. Every public act shall be made in these terms: "THE EMPEROR I. OF HAYTI, AND COMMANDER IN CHIEF OF THE ARMY BY THE GRACE OF GOD, AND THE CONSTITUTIONAL LAW OF THE STATE."

Of the Council of State.

38. The Generals of Division and of Brigade, are of right members of the Council of State, and they compose it.

Of the Ministers

39. There shall be in the Empire two ministers and a secretary of state. The ministers of finances having the department of the interior, and the minister of war having the marine department.

40-44. [Interior regulations respecting the ministry.]

Of the Tribunals.

45. No one can interfere with the right which every individual has of being judged amicably by arbitrators of his own choosing whose decisions shall be acknowledged legal.

46. There shall be a justice of peace in each commune. Any suit amounting to more than one hundred dollars shall not come within his cognizance. And when the parties cannot conciliate themselves at his tribunal, they may appeal to the tribunals of their respective districts.

47. There shall be six tribunals established in the cities hereafter designated, viz. At St. Marc, at the Cape, at Port au Prince, Aux Cayes, Lanse-a-Vaux, and Port-de-Paix... The Emperor determines their organization, their number, their competence and the territory forming the district of each. These tribunals take cognizance of all affairs purely civil.

48. Military crimes are submitted to special councils and to particular forms of judgement.

49. Particular laws shall be made for the national transactions, and respecting the civil officers of the state.

Of Worship

50. The law admits of no predominant religion.

51. The freedom of worship is tolerated.

52. The state does not provide for the maintenance of any

religious institution, nor or any minister.

Of the Administration

53. There shall be in each military division a principal administration, whose organization and inspection belongs essentially to the minister of finances.

General Dispositions.

Act. 1. To the Emperor and Empress belong the choice, the salary, and the maintenance of the persons composing their court.

2. After the decease of the reigning Emperor, when a revision of the constitution shall have been judged necessary, the council of state will assemble for that purpose, and shall be presided by the oldest member.

3. The crimes of high treason, the dilapidations of the ministers and generals shall be judged by a special council called and presided by the emperor.

4. The armed force is essentially obedient: no armed body can deliberate.

5. No person shall be judged without having been legally heard in his defense.

6. The house of every citizen is an inviolable asylum.

7. It cannot be entered but in case of conflagration, inundation, reclamation from the interior, or by virtue of an order from the emperor, or from any other authority legally constituted.

8. He deserves death who gives it to his fellow.

9. Every judgment to which the pain of death or corporal punishment is annexed shall not be carried into execution until it has been confirmed by the emperor.

10. Theft shall be punished according to the circumstances which may have preceded, accompanied or followed it.

11. Every stranger inhabiting the territory of Hayti shall be, equally with the Haytians, subject to the correctional and criminal laws of the country.

12. All property which formerly belonged to any white Frenchmen, is incontestably and of right confiscated to the

use of the state.

13. Every Haytian, who, having purchased property from a white Frenchman, may have paid part of the purchase money stipulated in the act of sale, shall be responsible to the domains of the state for the remainder of the sum due.

14. Marriage is an act purely civil, and authorized by the government.

15. The law authorises (sic) divorce in all cases which shall have been previously provided for and determined.

16. A particular law shall be issued concerning children born out of wedlock.

17. Respect for the chiefs, subordination and discipline are rigorously necessary.

18. A penal code shall be published and severely observed.

19. Within each military division a public school shall be established for the instruction of youth.

20. The national colours shall be black and red.

21. Agriculture, as it is the first, the most noble, and the most useful of all the arts, shall be honored and protected.

22. Commerce, the second source of the prosperity of states, will not admit of any impediment; it ought to be favored and specially protected.

23. In each military division a tribunal of commerce shall be found, whose members shall be chosen by the Emperor from the class of merchants.

24. Good faith and integrity in commercial operations shall be religiously maintained.

25. The government assures safety and protections to neutral nations and friends who may be desirous of establishing a commercial intercourse with this island, they conforming to the regulations and customs of the country.

26. The counting houses and the merchandize of foreigners shall be under the safeguard and guarantee of the state.

27. There shall be national festivals for celebrating independence, the birth day of the emperor and his august spouse, that of agriculture and of the constitution.

28. At the first firing of the alarm gun, the cities will disappear and the nation rise.

We, the undersigned, place under the safeguard of the magistrates, fathers and mothers of families, the citizens, and the army the explicit and solemn covenant of the sacred rights of man and the duties of the citizen.

We recommend it to our successors, and present it to the friends of liberty, to philanthropists of all countries, as a signal pledge of the Divine Bounty, who in the course of his immortal decrees, has given us an opportunity of breaking our fetters, and of constituting ourselves a people, free civilized and independent.

Signed

H. Christophe, & (as before)

Having seen the present constitution:

We, Jacques Dessalines, Emperor I of Hayti, and Commander in Chief of the Army, by the grace of God, and the constitutional law of the state, Accept it wholly and sanction it, that it may receive, with the least possible delay, its full and entire execution throughout the whole of our Empire.

And we swear to maintain it and to cause it to be observed in it integrity to the last breath of our life.

At the Imperial Palace of Dessalines, the 20th May 1805 second year of the Independence of Hayti, and of our reign the first.

DESSALINES

By the Emperor, Juste Chanlatte, Sec. Gen.